Culinary Arts Institute

The Cookie Jar

Featured in cover photo:
a. **Holiday String-Ups, 76**
b. **Swedish Jelly Slices, 87**
c. **Chocolate Chip Cookies, 12**
d. **Sugared Cocoa Delights, 46**
e. **Double Daisies, 60**
f. **Layered Chocolate Confections, 25**

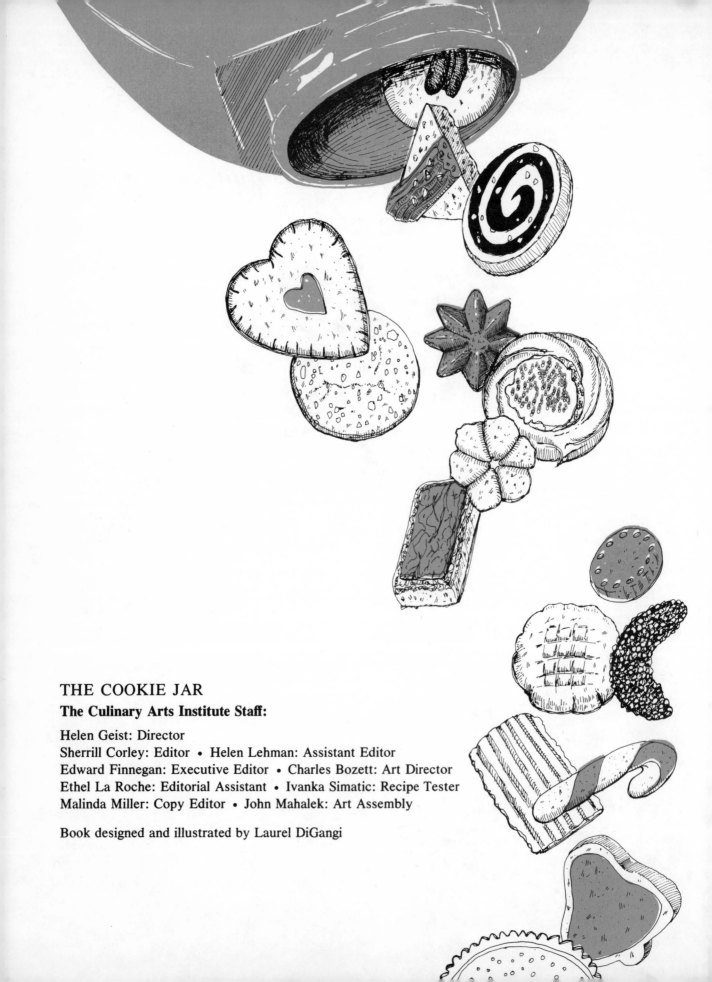

THE COOKIE JAR

The Culinary Arts Institute Staff:

Helen Geist: Director
Sherrill Corley: Editor • Helen Lehman: Assistant Editor
Edward Finnegan: Executive Editor • Charles Bozett: Art Director
Ethel La Roche: Editorial Assistant • Ivanka Simatic: Recipe Tester
Malinda Miller: Copy Editor • John Mahalek: Art Assembly

Book designed and illustrated by Laurel DiGangi

The Cookie Jar

Culinary Arts Institute

1727 South Indiana Avenue, Chicago, Illinois 60616

Culinary Arts Institute

1727 South Indiana Avenue, Chicago, Illinois 60616

Library of Congress Catalog Card Number: 76-41576
International Standard Book Number: 0-8326-0562-X
International Standard Book Number (Hard Cover): 0-8326-0563-8

PHOTO ACKNOWLEDGMENTS
American Dairy Association
American Spice Trade Association; Bob Scott Studios
C and H Sugar Kitchen; Diamond Walnut Growers, Inc.
The Quaker Oats Company

Introduction

Lucky is the kitchen with a well-stocked cookie jar. A cookie can appease a ravenous after-school appetite, provide a quick dessert, and heal everything from hurt feelings to a skinned knee. Just the aroma of cookies baking is enough to lift most spirits!

Cookies that are homemade offer a dimension of luxury. A generous portion of loving care goes in with the fresh ingredients—a winning combination that makes the baking time well worth the taking.

Very often, a budding cook chooses cookie baking for the beginning project. When that first pan of brownies emerges from the oven, the sense of accomplishment is something to savor—along with the thrill of that first bite!

Teenagers, in a hurry to grow up, like to think they have outgrown most childish interests. But few want to give up cookie making. They find it's a great party project; one that lets everybody get into the act. Cookie baking provides refreshments and entertainment, all rolled into one.

When a baby is ready to switch to do-it-yourself feeding, Mother may oblige with a cookie. It's perfect finger food. There is nothing to spill or splash; and even if it drops, no matter. That's the way the cookie crumbles.

Of course, cookies can go fancy. A rosette, deep-fat fried on a fancy iron, or a continental florentine, is sophisticated enough to conclude a gourmet dinner. And they are far less caloric than many three-tiered dessert productions! Cookies can be baked ahead of a party and will keep for weeks, if properly stored. And if proper security measures are taken, of course.

Nobody knows for sure who invented the cookie, but we're told that it started out as a test batch by a cake baker. A little dab was baked before the cake to see if the oven temperature was right—ancient equipment lacking the reliable controls of modern ovens. When the trial heat became as popular as the main event, bakers decided that cookies had earned a rightful place of their own. Dutch bakers called them "koekje," which means "little cake," and our own word "cookie" evolved.

In making this collection, the home economists at the CULINARY ARTS INSTITUTE have gathered together some of the world's most famous and beloved cookie recipes. Opening with a section for beginners, the following chapters are grouped by method. All the bar cookies are in one section; the drop cookies are in another, all those that are molded, refrigerated, or pressed are in still another, and so on. Other chapters include cookies with Old World ties, and cookies for the holidays.

The CULINARY ARTS INSTITUTE has a unique vantage point for making this selection of cookie recipes, as they have been supplying American homemakers with some of their favorite recipes since 1936. CULINARY ARTS INSTITUTE recipes have all been prepared and tasted in their test kitchen, so results are failure-proof.

Beginning cooks will find basic recipes: "cookies to learn by." Seasoned cooks will find everything from the old stand-bys to elegant specialties that require virtuosity. For everyone, this is a full spectrum of classic recipes to consult whenever the occasion calls for cookies.

Contents

Cookies to Learn By

Can you remember the first recipe you ever made? Most likely it was something you loved to eat—cookies, perhaps. Beginners usually like to start out with something familiar. And if there is a treat in store at the end of the job, so much the better! ¶ Few children need to be coaxed to learn to cook. Your budding chef has been watching you go about meal making ever since his first glimpse from the playpen.

You may have even given him an old pan and spoon to rattle while you worked.

Preschoolers can help out with little jobs such as providing the thumb for the thumbprint cookies. And they can do other related, but not strictly cooking things, while Mother cooks. A recipe that is great for a young child to shape and knead is this:

2 cups flour
1 cup salt
1 cup water

Combine the flour and salt in a big bowl, then add water gradually, stirring as you add. Knead until smooth. Then let Junior turn all his creativity loose. If he can manage a rolling pin, let him roll out the dough and cut shapes with a cookie cutter. If it's near holiday time, make a small hole at the top of the cut-out shapes to run a string through, and hang them for decorations. Either bake the shapes or let them dry to hardness. Unused dough can be put in a plastic bag and refrigerated for up to five days.

With this experience behind him, the school-age child will soon be ready and able to tackle the real thing. The first few times, you'll want to supervise closely, but once you feel he is able, let him assume the major responsibility. It's far more fun for him to feel that he did it all himself.

Naturally, you'll steer him to the simplest recipes first. Have him read through the one he chooses before he starts baking. That may take patience for the eager beginner, but it pays off. Help him line up ingredients as he reads. Then there's no possibility of running out of a necessary ingredient at the critical moment.

Safety will be your major concern as your child learns to cook. Don't be overly concerned about tidiness at first; you could throw his enthusiasm out with the dishwater. But pointers on how to handle a knife and potholders are essential. The first few times your child bakes, man the oven for him. Moving pans in and out can be tricky.

Removing the cookies from the pan should be assigned to a grownup at first, too. Explain that most cookies need a minute or two to firm up. But don't wait too long, or the cookies may harden to the pan. (Should this happen, slip the pan back in the oven for a minute or two.)

Let baking be fun, and you'll launch your child on a lifetime of cooking enjoyment.

Moravian Scotch Cakes

Bright colors in rich assortment are a feature of the famous bountiful tables of the Pennsylvania Dutch folk. These traditional cookies are as big as their hearts, as gaily colorful as Mom's aprons, and as tender as a maedle's (maiden's) blush!

4 cups sifted all-purpose flour
½ cup sugar
2 teaspoons caraway seed
1½ cups butter

1. Combine flour, sugar, and caraway seed in a bowl. Cut in butter until mixture becomes a soft dough (requires working beyond the stage when particles are the size of rice kernels); shape into a ball.
2. Roll a third of dough at a time ¼ inch thick on a floured surface. Cut into 2-inch squares. Transfer to lightly greased cookie sheets.
3. Bake at 325°F about 20 minutes.
4. Cool cookies; spread with Snowy Icing, *below*, and sprinkle with **colored sugar.**

About 3½ dozen cookies

Snowy Icing

1 cup sugar
¼ cup water
Few grains salt
1 egg white
1 teaspoon vanilla extract

1. Mix the sugar, water, and salt in a small saucepan; stir over low heat until sugar is dissolved.
2. Cook without stirring until mixture spins a 2-inch thread (about 230°F) when a small amount is dropped from a spoon.
3. Beat egg white until stiff, not dry, peaks are formed. Continue beating egg white while pouring hot syrup over it in a steady thin stream. After all the syrup is added, continue beating until icing is very thick and forms rounded peaks (holds shape).
4. Blend in extract.

About 2½ cups icing

Hermits

These old-fashioned spicy raisin cookies are a part of our New England heritage.

1 cup dark seedless raisins
2½ cups sifted all-purpose flour
¾ teaspoon baking soda
½ teaspoon salt
1 teaspoon ground cinnamon
½ teaspoon ground nutmeg
⅛ teaspoon ground cloves
¾ cup butter
1½ cups firmly packed brown sugar
3 eggs
1 cup walnuts, chopped

1. Pour **2 cups boiling water** over raisins in a saucepan and bring to boiling; pour off water and drain raisins on absorbent paper. Coarsely chop raisins and set aside.
2. Sift flour, baking soda, salt, and spices together and blend thoroughly; set aside.
3. Cream butter; add brown sugar gradually, beating until fluffy. Add eggs, one at a time, beating thoroughly after each addition.
4. Add dry ingredients in fourths, mixing until blended after each addition. Stir in raisins and walnuts.
5. Drop by teaspoonfuls 2 inches apart onto lightly greased cookie sheets.
6. Bake at 400°F about 7 minutes.

About 8 dozen cookies

Ginger Shortbread

1½ cups sifted all-purpose flour
1 teaspoon ground ginger
¼ teaspoon salt
½ cup butter or margarine
⅓ cup firmly packed brown sugar
1 tablespoon heavy cream

1. Sift flour, ginger, and salt together; set aside.
2. Cream butter; add brown sugar gradually, beating well. Add flour mixture gradually, mixing until well blended. Stir in cream.
3. Divide dough into halves. Place on an ungreased cookie sheet. Flatten into rounds about ½ inch thick. Mark into wedges. Flute the edges and prick centers with a fork.
4. Bake at 350°F about 20 minutes.
5. While still warm, cut into wedges.

2 shortbread rounds

Molasses Butter Balls

1 cup butter
½ teaspoon vanilla extract
¼ cup molasses
2 cups sifted all-purpose flour
½ teaspoon salt
2 cups pecans, finely chopped

1. Cream butter with extract; add molasses and beat well.
2. Blend flour and salt; add in fourths to creamed mixture, mixing until blended after each addition. Stir in the pecans.
3. Shape dough into 1-inch balls; place on lightly greased cookie sheets.
4. Bake at 350°F 12 to 15 minutes.
5. Cool slightly; roll in **confectioners' sugar.**

About 5 dozen cookies

Beginner Brownies

½ cup (1 stick) butter or margarine
2 squares (1 ounce each)
   unsweetened chocolate
1 cup sugar
2 eggs
1 teaspoon vanilla extract
¾ cup all-purpose flour
½ cup chopped nuts (optional)

1. In the top of a double boiler, melt butter and chocolate together over water that is simmering, not boiling.
2. Meanwhile, use the butter wrapper to grease a square 8-inch baking pan. Shake in a little flour, then shake out excess.
3. When butter and chocolate have melted, remove the top from the double boiler and set it on the counter top to cool. Add sugar.
4. When mixture is room temperature, blend in eggs one at a time, beating well. Do this by hand or use the electric mixer.
5. Add vanilla extract. Stir in flour and if desired, chopped nuts. Stir only until ingredients are well mixed. Spread batter in prepared pan.
6. Bake at 350°F for 30 minutes, no longer. Remove from oven and place on a rack to cool. When room temperature, cut into 16 squares.

16 brownies

Coconut Almond Logs

1 package (8 ounces) cream cheese
½ teaspoon vanilla extract
3 cups sifted confectioners' sugar
2 cups uncooked quick-cooking rolled oats
½ cup flaked coconut
½ cup slivered blanched almonds, chopped
1 cup flaked coconut, toasted*

1. Beat cream cheese with vanilla extract until creamy. Add confectioners' sugar gradually, beating until blended. Stir in oats, ½ cup coconut, and almonds.
2. Shape mixture into 2-inch logs. Roll logs in toasted coconut to coat. Chill until firm. Store in refrigerator.

About 3 dozen

*To toast coconut, spread coconut in a shallow pan and put into a 350°F oven for 5 to 10 minutes, or until lightly toasted; stir several times.

Chocolate Chip Cookies

1 cup sifted all-purpose flour
½ teaspoon baking powder
⅛ teaspoon baking soda
⅛ teaspoon salt
½ cup butter
1 teaspoon vanilla extract
¾ cup firmly packed light brown sugar
1 egg
1 package (6 ounces) semisweet chocolate pieces
½ cup chopped nuts

1. Blend flour, baking powder, baking soda, and salt.
2. Cream butter with vanilla extract. Add brown sugar gradually, creaming well. Add egg and beat thoroughly. Mix in dry ingredients, then chocolate pieces and nuts.
3. Drop batter by teaspoonfuls onto ungreased baking sheets.
4. Bake at 375°F 10 to 12 minutes.
5. Cool cookies on wire racks.

About 4 dozen cookies

Hazelnut Balls (Haselnuss Bällchen)

A German cookie.

2 egg whites
1 cup sugar
1½ cups (about 6 oz.) hazelnuts (filberts), grated

1. Beat egg whites until frothy; add sugar gradually, beating constantly until stiff peaks are formed.
2. Sprinkle hazelnuts over the egg whites and gently fold together just until blended.
3. Drop mixture by teaspoonfuls onto lightly greased cookie sheets. If necessary, work over each portion with the back of a spoon to round it.
4. Bake at 300°F about 25 minutes.
5. With a spatula, carefully remove cookies from cookie sheets to wire racks.

About 4 dozen cookies

Overnight Cookies (Hoide Kager)

A Danish cookie.

2¼ cups sifted all-purpose flour
1 cup sugar
1 cup butter
½ cup cream
¼ teaspoon vanilla extract
⅛ teaspoon lemon extract

1. Sift flour and sugar together; cut in butter until particles are the size of rice kernels.
2. Combine cream and extracts; add gradually to flour mixture, mixing with a fork until well blended.
3. Chill dough until easy to handle.
4. Shape into two 1½-inch rolls. Wrap and chill overnight.
5. Cut each roll into ⅛- or ¼-inch slices. Transfer slices to ungreased cookie sheets.
6. Bake at 350°F 9 to 12 minutes.

6 to 8 dozen cookies

Cinnamon Pecan Bars

½ cup butter
1 cup sugar
1 egg
½ cup all-purpose flour
1¼ teaspoons ground cinnamon
¼ teaspoon salt
1 cup pecans, finely chopped

1. Cream butter; add sugar gradually, creaming thoroughly. Add egg and beat until fluffy.
2. Sift flour, cinnamon, and salt together. Add to creamed mixture and mix until blended. Stir in pecans. Turn into a greased 8×8×2-inch baking pan and spread evenly.
3. Bake at 350°F 40 minutes.
4. Cut into small bars while still warm; coat with **confectioners' sugar.**

About 2½ dozen cookies

Mom's Sultanas

1 cup sifted all-purpose flour
¾ teaspoon baking powder
⅛ teaspoon baking soda
⅛ teaspoon salt
⅔ cup butter
2 teaspoons grated lemon peel
½ cup sugar
1 egg
2 tablespoons lemon juice
1 cup uncooked rolled oats
½ cup golden raisins

1. Sift flour, baking powder, baking soda, and salt together; set aside.
2. Cream butter with lemon peel; add sugar gradually, creaming until fluffy. Add egg and beat thoroughly.
3. Alternately add dry ingredients with lemon juice, mixing until blended after each addition. Stir in rolled oats and raisins.
4. Drop by teaspoonfuls about 2 inches apart onto lightly greased cookie sheets.
5. Bake at 375°F 12 to 15 minutes.

About 4 dozen cookies

Pecan Dainties

1 egg white
½ cup firmly packed brown sugar, sifted
1¼ cups chopped pecans
1½ tablespoons flour

1. Beat egg white until frothy. Add brown sugar gradually, beating until very stiff peaks are formed. Fold in pecans and flour.
2. Drop by teaspoonfuls 2 inches apart onto lightly greased cookie sheets; shape into balls with the back of a spoon.
3. Bake at 350°F about 10 minutes.

About 4 dozen cookies

Surprise Bars

A crunchy, nutty-rich top layer disguises a delectable bottom layer . . . the surprise element of this cookie bar.

1 oz. (1 sq.) unsweetened chocolate
½ cup graham cracker crumbs
2 tablespoons butter, melted
½ cup butter or margarine
½ teaspoon vanilla extract
½ cup sugar
1 egg
¾ cup sifted all-purpose flour
⅛ teaspoon baking soda
⅛ teaspoon salt
¼ cup dairy sour cream
¾ cup walnuts, coarsely chopped

1. Melt chocolate and set aside to cool.
2. Blend crumbs and melted butter; set aside.
3. Cream the ½ cup butter with the extract; add sugar gradually, beating until fluffy. Add egg and beat thoroughly.
4. Sift flour, baking soda, and salt together; add alternately to creamed mixture with sour cream, mixing until blended after each addition.
5. Divide mixture in half; blend cooled chocolate into one portion.
6. Turn chocolate mixture into a greased 8×8×2-inch baking pan and spread evenly. Cover with the crumbs and press lightly.
7. Stir walnuts into remaining portion; drop by spoonfuls over crumbs and carefully spread evenly.
8. Bake at 375° 25 to 30 minutes.
9. While warm, cut into bars.

2½ dozen cookies

Bar Cookies

Among the easiest of cookies are the bars. If they aren't the learner's first choice, they usually follow along very soon. Brownies, for one, are not only toothsome, they are simplicity itself. They require no shaping, no cutting, no molding—you simply whip up a batter, then pour it into the pan. ¶ But just as the finest art often follows the simplest lines, exquisite desserts can be built on a bar cookie base. In this section, both the easy bars and fancy variations are included.

Rumor has it that the first brownies were a chocolate cake that went wrong. Perhaps some forgetful cook left out the leavener. Whether intentional or not, it was a stroke of genius. One of those rareties, a really new recipe, was born.

Cookies that are made by spreading dough into a pan, baking, and then cutting it into shapes, belong to the bar family. But as with all themes, this one is open to many variations. Flavorings, colorings, and ingredients that lend both flavor and texture can be stirred into the batter.

The main tip to the bar baker is to use restraint when stirring. Overmixing makes for a hard top and tough texture throughout. Better to stir by hand only until ingredients are well-mixed than to overdo it with the mixer.

And don't fudge on pan size. If the recipe calls for an 8×8-inch pan, don't make do with a 9-incher, or the bars will be thin and overbaked.

There is no simple test to tell you when the bars are baked; it's best to go by the baking time in the recipe. Where a range is given, it's to allow for the difference in individual ovens.

Cut the bars when they've cooled to room temperature. They may crumble if cut when still hot.

Experienced bar bakers like to add improvisations of their own. In this chapter you will encounter many adaptations and variations. Brownies, for example, can run the gamut from Fudgy Brownies to the Layered Chocolate Confections that boast a rich brandy-chocolate topping.

But even though all brownies may be bars, not all bars are brownies. In this collection of recipes you will find varieties with everything from fruits to nuts. Here are a couple of baker's dozens—and more—to whet your appetite.

And if you're inclined to improvise, you needn't stop with the baking. You can add toppings of pudding or ice cream. You can embellish even more with toppings of fresh fruit or sauces in fifty nifty flavors. There is hardly an end to the possibilities.

Bar cookies are good travelers. You can take them along on a picnic, right in the pan in which they were baked. Just cut and pass, and let everyone help himself.

Date Perfections

¾ cup sifted all-purpose flour
¾ teaspoon baking powder
¼ teaspoon salt
2 eggs
¾ cup sugar
1½ cups dates, finely chopped
1 cup pecans, finely chopped
Lemon Glaze, *page 20*

1. Sift flour, baking powder, and salt together; set aside.
2. Beat eggs and sugar together until mixture is thick and piled softly.
3. Fold in dry ingredients, dates, and pecans until blended. Turn into a greased 11×7×1½-inch baking pan and spread evenly into corners.
4. Bake at 325°F 30 to 35 minutes.
5. Immediately brush surface with Lemon Glaze. While warm, cut into squares.

About 2 dozen cookies

Note: Dried figs or apricots may be used instead of dates.

Choco-Oat Bars

½ cup butter
½ cup peanut butter
1½ teaspoons vanilla extract
¾ cup firmly packed brown sugar
1 cup sifted all-purpose flour
½ teaspoon baking soda
¼ teaspoon salt
¼ cup water
1 cup uncooked rolled oats
6 oz. semisweet chocolate pieces

1. Cream butter with peanut butter and extract thoroughly; add brown sugar gradually, beating until fluffy.
2. Sift flour, baking soda, and salt together; add to creamed mixture alternately with water, mixing until blended after each addition. Stir in rolled oats.
3. Chill dough thoroughly.
4. Meanwhile, melt and cool chocolate.
5. Invert an 11×7×1½-inch baking pan onto a piece of waxed paper; mark around pan with a knife to form an outline without cutting through paper.
6. Divide the dough into halves; press half evenly into pan. Spread with cooled chocolate.
7. Pat remainder of dough evenly over marked oblong on waxed paper. Invert onto chocolate layer, press down gently and peel off paper.
8. Bake at 375°F 15 to 20 minutes.
9. Cool completely; cut into bars.

About 4½ dozen cookies

Peanut Butter Bars: Follow recipe for Choco-Oat Bars. Use a 15×10×1-inch jelly roll pan. Decrease brown sugar to ½ cup and add ½ **cup sugar.** Add **1 egg** to creamed mixture and beat thoroughly. Increase flour to 1¼ cups. Substitute 1½ **teaspoons baking powder** for baking soda. Omit water, oats, and chocolate pieces. Press all the dough into pan without chilling; bake. While warm, cut into bars.

Wheat-Flake Bars

2 cups whole wheat cereal flakes
2 cups sifted all-purpose flour
1 teaspoon baking powder
¾ cup firmly packed brown sugar
¾ cup plus 2 tablespoons butter or
   margarine, chilled
½ cup orange marmalade
   Glossy Orange Frosting, *below*
   Semisweet chocolate pieces

1. Mix cereal, flour, baking powder, and brown sugar in a bowl. Cut in butter until crumbly.
2. Press about two-thirds of the mixture in an even layer on the bottom of a 13×9×2-inch pan. Spread with marmalade; sprinkle remaining cereal mixture over marmalade.
3. Bake at 350°F about 30 minutes. Remove to a wire rack. Cool completely.
4. Frost with Glossy Orange Frosting. Cut into 3×1-inch bars. Decorate each bar with three semisweet chocolate pieces (points up).

3 dozen cookies

Glossy Orange Frosting: Beat **1 egg white** slightly; beat in **1½ cups confectioners' sugar**. Add **1 tablespoon melted butter** or **margarine**, **⅛ teaspoon salt**, **1 teaspoon vanilla extract**, and **¼ teaspoon orange extract**; beat until smooth. Blend in, one drop at a time, orange food coloring (a mixture of about **2 drops** of **red** and **6 drops** of **yellow**) until frosting is tinted a light orange.

About 1 cup frosting

Buttery Bitters Bars

An unusual cookie—few will recognize the interesting flavor of Angostura bitters which permeates it.

1 cup butter or margarine
½ cup sugar
3 cups fine graham cracker crumbs
   (about 3 doz. square crackers)
2 cups firmly packed brown sugar
1 tablespoon flour
1 teaspoon baking powder
1 cup flaked coconut
1 cup coarsely chopped walnuts
1 tablespoon Angostura bitters
3 eggs, well beaten

1. Cut butter into a mixture of the ½ cup sugar and the crumbs until thoroughly blended. Press firmly into two ungreased 9×9×2-inch baking pans. Set aside.
2. Blend the brown sugar, flour, and baking powder. Mix in coconut and walnuts.
3. Combine bitters with beaten eggs, add to brown sugar mixture and beat thoroughly. Spread evenly over layer in each pan.
4. Bake at 350°F 35 minutes, or until top layer is set.
5. Cool in pan on rack. While still warm, cut into small bars. Coat lightly with **confectioners' sugar.**

8 to 10 dozen bars

Note: If desired, cut in 3-inch squares (omit confectioners' sugar) and serve with whipped dessert topping, whipped cream, or ice cream.

Choco-Honey Chews

1¾ cups honey-flavored graham
   cracker crumbs
1 can (14 oz.) sweetened condensed
   milk
2 tablespoons honey
1½ teaspoons grated orange peel
2 tablespoons orange juice
1 cup semisweet chocolate pieces
¾ cup coarsely chopped pecans

1. Put crumbs into a bowl. Add the condensed milk, honey, and orange peel and juice; mix well. Stir in the chocolate pieces and pecans. Turn into a greased 13×9×2-inch baking pan and spread evenly.
2. Bake at 325°F 30 minutes.
3. While warm, cut into bars.

About 4 dozen cookies

Mint Diamonds

1 cup butter
1 teaspoon vanilla extract
1 cup firmly packed brown sugar
1 egg
2 cups sifted all-purpose flour
½ teaspoon baking powder
½ teaspoon salt
   Creamy Pastel Frosting, *below*
   Chocolate-Mint Glaze, *below*
½ cup pecans, chopped

1. Cream butter with extract; add brown sugar gradually, beating until fluffy. Add egg and beat thoroughly.
2. Sift flour, baking powder, and salt together; add to creamed mixture in fourths, mixing until blended after each addition. Turn mixture into ungreased 15×10×1-inch jelly roll pan and spread evenly.
3. Bake at 350°F 20 to 25 minutes; cool.
4. Spread the frosting quickly over cooled cookie base; spread glaze over frosting and sprinkle with nuts. Cool; cut into diamond shapes.

About 4 dozen cookies

Creamy Pastel Frosting

1½ cups sugar
½ cup cream
6 tablespoons butter
   Food coloring

1. Put sugar, cream, and butter into a heavy saucepan; stir over low heat to dissolve sugar. Increase heat and bring to boiling; stir occasionally.
2. Put candy thermometer in place; continue cooking without stirring to 234°F.
3. Remove from heat; cool to 110°F, or until just cool enough to hold pan on palm of hand; do not stir.
4. Using food coloring to harmonize with the color scheme for the special occasion, blend 1 or 2 drops into sugar mixture and beat until frosting is of spreading consistency.

About 1½ cups

Chocolate-Mint Glaze: Melt **6 ounces (1 cup) semisweet chocolate pieces** with **½ teaspoon mint extract** over hot water. Cool slightly.

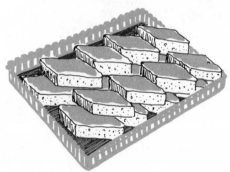

Graham Sensations

1¼ cups graham cracker crumbs
¼ cup sifted all-purpose flour
¼ teaspoon salt
1 can (14 oz.) sweetened condensed
   milk
¾ teaspoon vanilla extract
½ teaspoon grated lemon peel
½ cup flaked coconut
¾ cup coarsely chopped pecans
½ cup semisweet chocolate pieces

1. Blend crumbs, flour, and salt. Add condensed milk, extract, and lemon peel; mix well. Stir in remaining ingredients. Turn into a greased 13×9×2-inch baking pan and spread evenly.
2. Bake at 325°F 30 minutes.
3. While warm, cut into bars.

About 4 dozen cookies

Double-Quick Cookie Squares

30 square graham crackers
6 oz. semisweet chocolate pieces
½ cup grated coconut
1 can (14 oz.) sweetened condensed milk
½ cup chopped pecans

1. Crumble graham crackers into a bowl. Add chocolate pieces, coconut, and condensed milk; blend to moisten crackers. Turn into a lightly greased 9×9×2-inch baking pan. Top with pecans.
2. Bake at 325°F 30 minutes. (Cookies are moist and brown only slightly.)
3. Cool in pan on wire rack. Cut into squares.

3 dozen cookies

Glazed Cinnamon Bars

1 cup butter or margarine
1 cup firmly packed golden brown sugar
1 egg, separated
1¾ cups all-purpose flour
1 tablespoon cinnamon
Pinch salt
½ cup unsifted powdered sugar
1 cup walnuts, chopped

1. Put butter, brown sugar, and egg yolk into a bowl; beat until creamy. Blend flour, cinnamon, and salt; add to creamed mixture and mix well. Spread in an even layer in a lightly greased 15×10×1-inch jelly-roll pan.
2. Beat egg white until frothy. Stir in powdered sugar. Brush mixture over layer in pan. Sprinkle with walnuts.
3. Bake at 350°F 30 to 35 minutes. While still hot, cut into bars. Remove from pan and cool on wire racks.

4 dozen cookies

Peanut Butter Dreams

¼ cup butter
½ cup peanut butter
½ cup firmly packed light brown sugar
1 cup sifted all-purpose flour
2 eggs
1 teaspoon vanilla extract
1 cup firmly packed light brown sugar
⅓ cup sifted all-purpose flour
½ teaspoon baking powder
¾ cup flaked coconut
6 oz. semisweet chocolate pieces

1. Cream butter with peanut butter thoroughly; add ½ cup brown sugar gradually, beating until fluffy.
2. Add 1 cup flour in halves, mixing until blended after each addition. Press evenly into greased 9×9×2-inch baking pan.
3. Bake at 350°F 10 to 15 minutes, or until lightly browned.
4. Meanwhile, beat eggs, extract, and 1 cup brown sugar until thick. Add a mixture of ⅓ cup flour and the baking powder; beat until blended.
5. Stir in coconut and chocolate pieces. Spread evenly over partially baked layer in pan.
6. Return to oven and bake 30 minutes.
7. Cool completely and cut into squares or bars.

About 2 dozen cookies

Black Walnut Dreams

In this recipe, chopped pecans may be used instead of black walnuts with little loss of fine flavor.

2 tablespoons butter
5 tablespoons all-purpose flour
⅛ teaspoon baking soda
⅛ teaspoon salt
1 cup black walnuts, coarsely chopped
2 eggs
¾ teaspoon vanilla extract
¼ teaspoon lemon extract
1 cup firmly packed brown sugar

1. Melt butter in a 8×8×2-inch baking pan; set aside.
2. Sift flour, baking soda, and salt together; stir in walnuts; set aside.
3. Beat eggs and extracts; add brown sugar gradually, beating until very thick. Blend in dry ingredients.
4. Turn into pan over melted butter; do not stir.
5. Bake at 350°F 25 to 30 minutes.
6. While warm, cut into squares and roll in **sugar**.

16 cookies

Almond Awards

1 cup butter
2 teaspoons grated lemon peel
1 cup sugar
1 cup sifted all-purpose flour
½ teaspoon salt
1 cup almonds, finely chopped
½ cup heavy cream

1. Cream ½ cup of the butter with the lemon peel and ½ cup of the sugar. Blend flour and salt; add in halves, mixing until blended after each addition.
2. Turn into an 11×7×1½-inch baking pan and spread into an even layer.
3. Bake at 375°F 12 minutes.
4. Meanwhile, melt remaining ½ cup butter in a heavy saucepan; add almonds and remaining ½ cup sugar. Cook the mixture 3 minutes, stirring constantly.
5. Stir in cream and heat to boiling; cool slightly. Spoon topping over partially baked layer.
6. Return to oven and bake 20 minutes, or until light golden.
7. Cool completely; cut into squares or bars.

About 5 dozen cookies

Apricot Sours

This cookie makes a delicious dessert when cut into large squares and topped with sweetened whipped cream.

⅔ cup butter, chilled
1½ cups sifted all-purpose flour
1 egg
½ cup firmly packed light brown sugar
¼ teaspoon vanilla extract
½ cup finely snipped apricots, cooked*
½ cup pecans, chopped
Lemon Glaze, *below*

1. Cut butter into flour until particles are the size of rice kernels. Press mixture evenly and firmly into a 13×9×2-inch baking pan.
2. Bake at 350°F 15 minutes.
3. Meanwhile, beat egg, brown sugar, and extract until thick; stir in a mixture of apricots and pecans.
4. Spread evenly over partially baked layer in pan.
5. Return to oven and bake about 20 minutes, or until lightly browned.
6. Remove from oven and immediately spread Lemon Glaze over top. When cool, cut into bars.

About 4 dozen cookies

*Put snipped apricots into a heavy saucepan with a small amount of water (3 to 4 tablespoons). Cover tightly and cook over low heat about 10 minutes, or until apricots are soft and liquid is absorbed. Cool.

Note: If packaged dried apricots are extremely soft, it may not be necessary to cook the apricots.

Lemon Glaze: Blend ¾ cup confectioners' sugar with 2 tablespoons lemon juice.

Frosted Ginger Bars

Bars:
- ½ cup butter or margarine
- ½ cup firmly packed brown sugar
- 1 egg
- ½ cup molasses
- 2 cups complete pancake mix
- 1½ teaspoons ginger
- 1½ teaspoons cinnamon
- ½ cup water

Frosting:
- 2 packages (3 ounces each) cream cheese
- 2 cups sifted confectioners' sugar
- 2 tablespoons lemon juice
- 1 tablespoon grated lemon peel

1. For bars, beat butter and brown sugar together until creamy. Add egg and beat well. Blend in molasses.
2. Blend pancake mix, ginger, and cinnamon; add to creamed mixture. Blend in water.
3. Turn batter into a greased and floured 15×10×1-inch jelly-roll pan and spread evenly.
4. Bake at 350°F about 20 minutes. Cool in pan on wire rack.
5. For frosting, beat cream cheese until fluffy. Add confectioners' sugar gradually, creaming until well mixed. Beat in lemon juice. Spread frosting over cooled bars. Sprinkle with grated lemon peel. Chill until frosting is set.
6. Cut into bars.

About 4 dozen cookies

Dream Bars DeLuxe

- 1 cup sifted all-purpose flour
- 3 tablespoons confectioners' sugar
- ½ cup butter or margarine, softened
- 2 eggs
- 1½ teaspoons vanilla extract
- 1½ cups firmly packed light brown sugar
- 2 tablespoons flour
- ¼ teaspoon baking powder
- ⅛ teaspoon salt
- ¾ cup walnuts, chopped
- ½ cup flaked coconut

1. Blend 1 cup flour, confectioners' sugar, and butter. Press evenly into an 11×7×1½-inch baking pan.
2. Bake at 350°F 20 minutes; remove pan to wire rack.
3. Meanwhile, beat eggs with extract and brown sugar until thick.
4. Blend in a mixture of 2 tablespoons flour, baking powder, and salt; mix in ½ cup of the walnuts and ¼ cup coconut.
5. Spread evenly over partially baked layer in pan and sprinkle with a mixture of remaining nuts and coconut.
6. Return to oven and bake 25 minutes.
7. Cool completely; cut into bars.

About 3 dozen cookies

Chewy Butterscotch Bars

- **Topping,** *below*
- 1⅓ cups sifted cake flour
- 2 teaspoons baking powder
- 1 teaspoon salt
- 2 cups firmly packed brown sugar
- ½ cup corn oil
- 2 teaspoons vanilla extract
- 2 eggs
- 1 cup coarsely chopped pecans
- 1 cup flaked coconut

1. Prepare Topping; set over simmering water.
2. Sift flour, baking powder, and salt together; set aside.
3. Beat brown sugar, corn oil, and extract; add eggs, one at a time, beating thoroughly after each addition.
4. Stir in flour mixture until blended. Mix in pecans and coconut.
5. Turn into a well-greased 15×10×1-inch jelly roll pan and spread into corners. Drizzle hot topping over entire surface.
6. Bake at 350°F 30 minutes.
7. Cool 30 minutes in pan, cut into bars, and remove from pan.

About 2½ dozen cookies

Topping: Blend **¾ cup firmly packed brown sugar, 2 tablespoons butter, 3 tablespoons cream or evaporated milk, and ¼ cup dark corn syrup** in a saucepan. Cook over medium heat, stirring occasionally, to 234°F. Remove from heat; blend in **1 teaspoon vanilla extract.**

About ⅔ cup

Fudgy Brownies

Fudge Sauce, *below*
½ cup butter
1½ oz. (1½ sq.) unsweetened chocolate
2 eggs
1 cup sugar
¾ cup sifted all-purpose flour
½ teaspoon baking powder
⅛ teaspoon salt
¾ cup pecans, coarsely chopped

1. Prepare Fudge Sauce; set aside.
2. Melt butter and chocolate together; set aside to cool.
3. Beat eggs and sugar until thick and piled softly; add cooled chocolate mixture and beat until blended.
4. Sift together flour, baking powder, and salt; add in halves to chocolate mixture, mixing until blended after each addition.
5. Turn half of batter into a greased 9×9×2-inch baking pan and spread evenly.
6. Pour half of Fudge Sauce evenly over batter; remove remaining sauce from heat but allow to stand over hot water.
7. Spread remaining batter evenly over sauce.
8. Bake at 350°F 35 to 40 minutes.
9. Set on wire rack 5 minutes; top with remaining sauce; sprinkle with pecans.
10. Broil 4 inches from source of heat 1 to 2 minutes, or until entire top is bubbly; do not allow sauce to burn. Cool completely before cutting into squares.

3 dozen cookies

Fudge Sauce

⅓ cup undiluted evaporated milk
⅓ cup sugar
4 teaspoons water
½ oz. (½ sq.) unsweetened chocolate, grated
1½ teaspoons butter
¼ teaspoon vanilla extract
⅛ teaspoon salt

1. Combine evaporated milk, sugar, and water in the top of a double boiler; stirring constantly, bring to boiling. Boil 3 minutes.
2. Remove from heat; blend in remaining ingredients.
3. Set over simmering water until needed.

About ½ cup sauce

Double Chocolate Squares: Follow recipe for Fudgy Brownies. Omit Fudge Sauce. Increase chocolate to 2 ounces (2 squares). After final addition of ingredients stir in pecans. Omit broiling; cool completely. If desired, spread with Chocolate Glaze II, *below*; decreasing butter to 1 tablespoon; arrange pecan halves on top. Leave in pan until glaze has become firm.

Chocolate Glaze II

4 oz. semisweet chocolate, melted
3 cups confectioners' sugar
4 teaspoons dark corn syrup
¼ cup cream
3 tablespoons boiling water
4 teaspoons butter
2 teaspoons vanilla extract

1. Mix all ingredients except extract in a heavy saucepan. Place over low heat and stir constantly until smooth; remove from heat.
2. Stir in extract; cool slightly.

Enough to glaze 3 dozen cookies

Luxury Mallow-Nut Brownies: Follow recipe for Double Chocolate Squares. Omit Chocolate Glaze and pecan halves. Melt **12 ounces semisweet chocolate pieces** and **2 tablespoons butter.** Cut **12 marshmallows** into quarters (or use 1⅓ cups miniature marshmallows) and stir into melted chocolate with ½ **cup coarsely chopped salted nuts,** such as pecans, pistachios, filberts, or almonds. Immediately spread over the baked brownies; cool.

Dinah Shore Brownies

When the fragrance of chocolate wafts from the kitchen of Dinah Shore, charming singing star and television personality, her family knows it's time for a batch of her famous brownies.

¾ **cup butter or margarine**
4 **oz. (4 sq.) unsweetened chocolate**
3 **eggs**
1½ **cups sugar**
1½ **teaspoons vanilla extract**
¾ **cup sifted all-purpose flour**
½ **cup coarsely chopped pecans**

1. Melt butter and chocolate together; cool.
2. Beat eggs, sugar, and extract until thick and piled softly. Add cooled chocolate mixture and beat until blended.
3. Mix in flour, then pecans. Turn into a greased 8×8×2-inch baking pan and spread evenly.
4. Bake at 350°F about 35 minutes.
5. Cut into squares.

About 2 dozen cookies

Hi-fi Brownies

½ **cup butter or margarine**
3 **oz. (3 sq.) unsweetened chocolate**
2 **eggs**
1 **cup sugar**
1 **teaspoon vanilla extract**
1¼ **cups sifted all-purpose flour**
½ **teaspoon baking powder**
½ **teaspoon salt**
1 **cup pecans, chopped**
5 **oz. marshmallows, cut in small pieces**
Chocolate Frosting, *below*

1. Melt butter and chocolate together; set aside to cool.
2. Beat eggs, sugar, and extract until thick and piled softly. Add cooled chocolate mixture and beat until blended.
3. Sift flour, baking powder, and salt together; add in thirds to egg-sugar mixture, mixing until blended after each addition. Stir in pecans. Turn into a greased 11×7×1½-inch baking pan and spread evenly.
4. Bake at 325°F 25 minutes.
5. Remove pan to wire rack. Immediately arrange marshmallow pieces over hot brownies.
6. Prepare Chocolate Frosting and spread over the brownies. Cut into 2×1-inch bars.

About 3 dozen cookies

Chocolate Frosting

½ **cup (3 oz.) semisweet chocolate pieces**
2 **tablespoons butter or margarine**
2 **cups confectioners' sugar**
⅛ **teaspoon salt**
½ **teaspoon vanilla extract**
3 **tablespoons double-strength coffee**
½ **cup flaked coconut**

1. Melt chocolate and butter together over hot water. Gradually add the confectioners' sugar, beating well after each addition.
2. Mix in salt and extract. Gradually add coffee, beating constantly. Continue to beat until mixture loses its gloss, about 2 minutes. Stir in coconut until well mixed.

About 1½ cups

Southern Brownies

Mrs. Andy Griffith, wife of the well-known TV star, contributed this recipe.

3 tablespoons shortening
2 oz. (2 sq.) unsweetened chocolate
2 egg yolks, well beaten
1 teaspoon vanilla extract
1 cup sugar
½ cup all-purpose flour
½ cup chopped nuts
2 egg whites

1. Melt shortening and chocolate together in a large saucepan; cool.
2. Stir in egg yolks, then extract, sugar, flour, and nuts.
3. Beat egg whites until stiff, not dry, peaks are formed. Blend into chocolate mixture.
4. Spread batter in a well-greased 8×8×2-inch pan.
5. Bake at 350°F 30 minutes, or until a wooden pick comes out clean.
6. Cool completely before cutting.

About 2 dozen cookies

Golden Nut Bars

1 cup finely crushed round scalloped crackers
½ cup pecans, finely chopped
1 cup sugar
1 teaspoon baking powder
3 egg whites
¼ teaspoon salt

1. Blend crumbs, pecans, sugar, and baking powder.
2. Beat egg whites and salt until stiff, not dry, peaks are formed; fold in the crumb mixture, a small amount at a time.
3. Turn into an ungreased 11×7×1½-inch baking pan and spread evenly.
4. Bake at 350°F 25 minutes.
5. Cool completely before cutting into bars.

About 3 dozen cookies

Mansion Squares

½ cup butter
1 teaspoon vanilla extract
¾ cup firmly packed brown sugar
1 egg
1 cup sifted all-purpose flour
½ teaspoon baking powder
⅛ teaspoon baking soda
⅛ teaspoon salt
6 oz. semisweet chocolate pieces

1. Cream butter with extract; add brown sugar gradually, beating until fluffy. Add egg; beat well.
2. Sift flour, baking powder, baking soda, and salt together; add in thirds to creamed mixture, mixing until blended after each addition. Turn into greased 11×7×1½-inch baking pan. Top with chocolate pieces.
3. Bake at 350°F about 30 minutes.
4. While warm, cut into squares.

About 2 dozen cookies

Nut Mansion Squares: Follow recipe for Mansion Squares. Substitute **1 cup coarsely chopped filberts** for semisweet chocolate pieces.

Chocolate-Nut Mansion Squares: Follow recipe for Mansion Squares. Top with chocolate pieces immediately after removing from oven rather than before baking. When chocolate is softened, spread evenly over surface. Sprinkle with **1 cup filberts,** coarsely chopped.

Layered Chocolate Confections

Chocolate Layer:
- ½ cup butter or margarine
- 2 oz. (2 sq.) unsweetened chocolate
- 2 eggs
- 1 cup sugar
- 1 teaspoon vanilla extract
- ½ cup sifted all-purpose flour
- ½ cup chopped salted pecans

Cream Layer:
- ½ cup heavy cream
- ⅓ cup butter or margarine
- 1½ cups sugar
- 2 tablespoons brandy
- 2 oz. (2 sq.) unsweetened chocolate, melted and cooled slightly

1. Chocolate Layer: Melt the butter and chocolate together; set aside to cool.
2. Beat eggs, sugar, and extract until thick and piled softly. Add cooled chocolate mixture and beat until blended. Stir in flour, then pecans. Turn into a greased 11×7×1½-inch baking pan and spread evenly.
3. Bake at 350°F about 25 minutes.
4. Cool in pan on wire rack.
5. Cream Layer: Combine cream, butter, and sugar in a heavy saucepan. Cook, stirring occasionally, over low heat until mixture reaches 236°F. Remove from heat; cool, undisturbed, to 110°F or just cool enough to hold pan on palm of hand. Turn into small bowl, add brandy, and beat until mixture is smooth and creamy. Spread on cooled chocolate layer. Chill slightly until top is firm to the touch. Spread melted chocolate over creamy layer. Chill thoroughly.
6. Cut into 1-inch squares. Place in bonbon cups to serve or pack in a gift box.

About 6 dozen confections

Note: A drop or two of **food coloring** may be blended with cream mixture to harmonize with various party color schemes.

Wheatfield Bars

- 2 cups graham cracker crumbs
- ½ cup wheat germ
- ¼ teaspoon salt
- 1 can (14 oz.) sweetened condensed milk
- 2 teaspoons vanilla extract
- 6 oz. semisweet chocolate pieces

1. Blend crumbs, wheat germ, and salt; mix in remaining ingredients.
2. Turn into lightly greased 8×8×2-inch baking pan and spread evenly.
3. Bake at 350°F about 35 minutes; avoid overbaking.
4. Cool; cut into bars.

About 1½ dozen cookies

Triple-Treat Walnut Bars

- ½ cup butter or margarine
- 1 package (3 ounces) cream cheese
- ½ cup firmly packed dark brown sugar
- 1 cup whole wheat flour
- ⅓ cup toasted wheat germ
- 1 package (6 ounces) semisweet chocolate pieces
- 2 eggs
- ½ cup honey
- ⅓ cup whole wheat flour
- ⅓ cup instant nonfat dry milk
- ¼ teaspoon salt
- ¼ teaspoon ground cinnamon
- ¼ teaspoon ground mace
- 1½ cups chopped walnuts

1. Cream butter, cheese, and sugar in a bowl until light. Add 1 cup whole wheat flour and wheat germ and mix until smooth. Turn into a greased 13×9×2-inch pan; spread evenly.
2. Bake at 375°F 15 to 18 minutes, until edges are very lightly browned and top is firm.
3. Remove from oven and sprinkle with chocolate. Let stand about 5 minutes, or until chocolate softens, then spread it evenly over baked layer.
4. Combine eggs and honey; beat just until well blended. Add ⅓ cup whole wheat flour, dry milk, salt, cinnamon, mace, and walnuts; mix well. Spoon over the chocolate.
5. Return to oven and bake 18 to 20 minutes, or until top is set. Cool in pan, then cut into bars or diamonds.

About 3 dozen cookies

Apricot Squares

8 ounces dried apricots, cut in small pieces
2 cups boiling water
1¼ cups sifted all-purpose flour
½ teaspoon baking soda
¼ teaspoon salt
½ cup firmly packed brown sugar
½ cup butter or margarine
1¼ cups uncooked rolled oats, quick cooking or old fashioned
½ cup chopped walnuts
⅓ cup honey

1. Put apricot pieces into a small bowl and pour boiling water over them; cover and let stand 20 minutes. Drain apricots and set aside.
2. Blend flour, baking soda, and salt in a bowl. Mix in brown sugar. Cut in butter. Add oats and mix well.
3. Turn half of oats mixture into a greased 8-inch square baking pan; press into an even layer. Spoon drained apricots over first layer. Sprinkle with nuts. Pour honey over all. Top with remaining oats mixture; press into an even layer.
4. Bake at 350°F 30 to 35 minutes.
5. Cool completely in pan. Cut into squares.

16 cookies

Lemon-Coconut Sours

⅓ cup butter, chilled
¾ cup sifted all-purpose flour
2 eggs
1 teaspoon grated lemon peel
½ teaspoon vanilla extract
1 cup firmly packed light brown sugar
¾ cup flaked coconut
½ cup pecans, coarsely chopped
Lemon Glaze, *page 20*

1. Cut butter into flour until thoroughly blended. Press evenly and firmly into an ungreased 13×9×2-inch baking pan.
2. Bake at 350°F 10 minutes.
3. Meanwhile, beat eggs, lemon peel, extract, and brown sugar until thick. Stir in coconut and pecans. Spread evenly over partially baked layer in pan.
4. Return to oven and bake about 20 minutes.
5. Immediately spread Lemon Glaze evenly over top. When cool, cut into bars or squares.

About 4 dozen cookies

Pineapple Bars: Follow recipe for Lemon-Coconut Sours. Substitute **unblanched almonds,** toasted and chopped, for pecans. Omit lemon peel and Lemon Glaze. Fold in **⅓ cup drained crushed pineapple** with coconut and almonds. Bake about 25 minutes.

Peanut Blonde Brownies

½ cup chunk-style peanut butter
¼ cup butter or margarine
1 teaspoon vanilla extract
1 cup firmly packed light brown sugar
2 eggs
½ cup sifted all-purpose flour
1 cup chopped salted peanuts
Confectioners' sugar

1. Cream peanut butter with butter and extract. Gradually add brown sugar, beating well. Add eggs, one at a time, beating until fluffy after each addition.
2. Add flour in halves, mixing until blended after each addition. Stir in peanuts. Turn into a greased 8×8×2-inch baking pan and spread evenly.
3. Bake at 350°F 30 to 35 minutes.
4. Remove pan to wire rack to cool 5 minutes before cutting into 2-inch squares. Remove from pan and cool on rack. Sift confectioners' sugar over tops.

16 brownies

Crown Jewels

Toppings, *below*
1 cup butter or margarine
½ teaspoon grated orange peel
½ cup sugar
2 hard-cooked egg yolks, sieved
2 cups sifted all-purpose flour

1. Prepare Toppings.
2. Cream butter with orange peel. Gradually add sugar, beating until fluffy.
3. Blend in sieved hard-cooked egg yolks. Add flour in fourths, mixing well after each addition.
4. Press dough firmly onto bottom of ungreased 15×10×1-inch jelly roll pan.
5. Bake at 350°F 20 minutes.
6. While still warm, spread with Date Topping and then Candied Fruit Topping. Cool thoroughly and cut into fancy shapes.

About 3 dozen cookies

Date Topping: Mix **1 cup (about 7 ounces) pitted dates,** finely chopped, with ¼ **cup orange juice** in the top of a double boiler. Heat, covered, over simmering water 10 minutes, stirring occasionally; cool.

Candied Fruit Topping

½ lb. red and green candied pineapple, finely chopped (1⅔ cups)
¼ lb. candied red cherries, finely chopped (⅔ cup)
2 oz. candied orange peel, finely chopped (⅓ cup)
⅓ cup rum

Mix candied fruit with rum in the top of a double boiler. Heat, covered, over simmering water 30 minutes, stirring occasionally; cool slightly.

Aristocrats

A distinctive pecan topping is the praise-winning feature of these apricot cookies of French origin.

¾ cup butter
1 teaspoon vanilla extract
⅔ cup sugar
1 egg
2 cups sifted cake flour
⅔ cup apricot preserves
Pecan Topping

1. Cream butter with extract; add sugar gradually, creaming until fluffy. Add egg and beat thoroughly.
2. Add flour in fourths, mixing until blended after each addition.
3. Turn dough into a lightly greased 11×7×1½-inch baking pan and spread evenly. Spread the apricot preserves over dough.
4. Bake at 350°F 20 to 25 minutes, or until edges are lightly browned. Remove pan to wire rack (do not remove cookie layer from pan).
5. Prepare Pecan Topping and spread evenly over cooled cookie layer. Chill 2 to 3 hours.
6. Cut into strips, about 2½×¾-inch. Place strips about ½ inch apart on cookie sheets.
7. Bake at 375°F 15 minutes, or until topping is delicately browned.

About 4 dozen cookies

Pecan Topping: Beat **1 egg white** with ⅛ **teaspoon salt** until frothy. Add ⅔ **cup sugar** and **2 teaspoons flour** gradually, beating thoroughly after each addition. Beat until stiff peaks are formed. Fold in ⅔ **cup pecans,** finely chopped.

Spicy Walnut Diamonds

2½ cups sifted all-purpose flour
2 tablespoons cocoa
1½ teaspoons baking powder
1 teaspoon salt
½ teaspoon ground nutmeg
¼ teaspoon ground cloves
2 cups firmly packed brown sugar
3 eggs
½ cup honey
½ cup butter or margarine, melted
1½ cups chopped walnuts (1 cup medium and ½ cup fine)
½ cup confectioners' sugar
2 to 3 teaspoons milk

1. Blend flour, cocoa, baking powder, salt, nutmeg, and cloves.
2. Combine brown sugar and eggs in a large bowl; beat until well blended and light. Add honey, butter, and flour mixture and mix until smooth.
3. Stir in the 1 cup medium walnuts, and spread evenly in a greased 15×10×1-inch jelly-roll pan. Sprinkle the ½ cup fine walnuts over top.
4. Bake at 375°F about 20 minutes, or just until top springs back when touched lightly in center. Cool in pan.
5. Mix confectioners' sugar and enough milk to make a smooth, thin glaze. Spread over cooled layer. Cut into diamonds or bars.

About 4 dozen cookies

Luscious Lemon Bars

1 cup sifted all-purpose flour
¼ cup confectioners' sugar
½ cup butter, chilled
1 cup sugar
2 tablespoons flour
½ teaspoon baking powder
3 eggs, well beaten
½ cup unstrained lemon juice

1. Blend the 1 cup flour and confectioners' sugar in a bowl. Cut in the butter until blended. Firmly and evenly press into an ungreased 9×9×2-inch baking pan.
2. Bake at 350°F about 15 minutes.
3. Meanwhile, combine sugar, 2 tablespoons flour, and baking powder; blend into beaten eggs along with the lemon juice.
4. Pour mixture over crust in pan. Return to oven and bake 25 minutes.
5. Remove to wire rack to cool. Spread with a thin **confectioners' sugar icing** and top with **toasted sliced almonds.** Cut into bars.

About 3 dozen cookies

Cocoa Almond Bars Supreme

⅔ cup sifted all-purpose flour
⅓ cup Dutch process cocoa
½ teaspoon baking powder
¼ teaspoon salt
½ cup butter
¼ cup almond paste
1½ teaspoons vanilla extract
½ teaspoon almond extract
¾ cup sugar
1 egg
1 egg yolk
1 cup toasted blanched almonds, coarsely chopped
1 egg white
¼ teaspoon cream of tartar
¼ cup sugar

1. Blend flour, cocoa, baking powder, and salt; set aside.
2. Cream butter with almond paste and extracts until thoroughly blended. Add ¾ cup sugar gradually, beating until fluffy. Add egg and egg yolk; beat vigorously.
3. Mixing until blended after each addition, add dry mixture in thirds, then ½ cup of the almonds. Turn into a lightly greased 8×8×2-inch baking pan.
4. Beat egg white and cream of tartar until frothy. Add ¼ cup sugar gradually, continuing to beat until stiff peaks are formed. Fold in remaining almonds. Spread over batter in pan.
5. Bake at 350°F 35 to 40 minutes, or until meringue is lightly browned.
6. When thoroughly cooled cut into 2×1-inch bars.

2½ dozen cookies

Drop Cookies

Drop cookies come right after bars in the rank of easy bakers. Once the batter is made, all they need is a gentle nudge onto a baking sheet. ¶ The drop cookie is probably the forerunner of them all, if the tale is true that a test dab of cake batter originated the species. Other methods have been devised, but the drop cookie offers so much for so little effort that it has never been dropped from the baker's repertoire.

If you're after absolute perfection, use a measuring spoon to dip the cookie batter. Level it and push it off with a spatula. That's what test kitchens do, and it accounts for the fact that printed recipes give a higher yield than homemakers actually get when they scoop more generously.

Starting with a soft dough, the cookie will flatten out during baking, making a cookie that is thin and crisp. Cookies usually spread out during baking, so place them about two inches apart unless the recipe says otherwise.

Generally, it's just as easy to stir up a double batch of dough as it is to make a single recipe, if you anticipate heavy demands on the cookie jar. Just freeze the second half of the dough. Take it from the freezer about a half hour before shaping and baking.

Or you can shape the cookies first, slip them into the freezer on a baking sheet until hard, and then transfer them to freezer bags for storage up to six months. (Baked cookies can be frozen for up to twelve months.) When baking the shaped frozen cookie dough, just add about three minutes to the baking time. Or you can let the cookies come to room temperature before baking. Then bake as usual.

Cooks sometimes wonder why a range of times is given in a cookie recipe. The answer is that ovens vary, and rarely do two cooks get exactly the same results. It's best to start checking the cookies at the end of the minimum baking time, and let them go a little longer if they aren't quite done.

You can often tell by looking when the cookies are done. Most lose their glossy look, and light-colored cookies acquire a golden rim. You can also touch the baked cookie lightly in the center with your finger. If almost no imprint remains, it's probably done.

Drop cookies, like all other cookies, can be frozen for future enjoyment. Use a sturdy box and line it with transparent plastic wrap which will cling to the cookies and seal out air that would otherwise dry them out. Plastic freezer containers lined with plastic wrap work fine, too.

Then, let the unexpected guest turn up or a surprise gift need arise—it will find you unflustered, thanks to your frozen assets.

Potato Chip Cookies

1 cup butter or margarine
1½ teaspoons vanilla extract
¼ cup sugar
¼ cup packed brown sugar
1¾ cups sifted all-purpose flour
1 cup finely crushed potato chips

1. Cream butter with vanilla extract. Add sugars gradually, creaming thoroughly. Mix in flour, then potato chip crumbs.
2. Chill dough until easy to handle.
3. Shape dough into small balls and place on ungreased cookie sheets. Flatten cookies with a floured table fork.
4. Bake at 350°F 12 to 15 minutes.

4 to 4½ dozen cookies

Cookie Cigarettes

For these interesting delicacies (of French derivation), both cookies and filling may be prepared ahead and the cookies filled shortly before serving.

¼ cup egg whites
½ cup confectioners' sugar
⅓ cup sifted flour
3 tablespoons butter, melted and cooled
¾ teaspoon vanilla extract
Rich Chocolate Filling, *below*

1. Beat egg whites until frothy; add confectioners' sugar gradually, beating thoroughly after each addition; beat until stiff peaks are formed.
2. Fold in flour in halves. Blend in cooled butter and extract.
3. Quickly grease a preheated cookie sheet. Bake a trial cookie; if it is too brittle to roll, the batter needs a little more flour; if the cookie is thick and difficult to roll, add a little more cooled melted butter.
4. Drop mixture by heaping teaspoonfuls 4 inches apart onto hot cookie sheet; spread very thinly without making holes; bake only a few cookies at one time (they are difficult to roll when cool).
5. Bake at 400°F 2 to 3 minutes, or until edges are lightly browned.
6. Immediately remove from cookie sheet. Quickly roll each cookie around a pencil-thin wooden rod; place on wire rack. Remove rods when cooled.
7. Store in a tightly covered container.
8. Shortly before serving, using a pastry bag and decorating tube, fill cookies from both ends with Rich Chocolate Filling.
9. Dip in chopped **pistachio nuts** or **chocolate shot**.

About 2 dozen cookies

Note: These cookies may also be made using a krumkake iron. Spoon 1 teaspoonful of mixture onto heated iron, close iron, and bake for 1 minute over medium heat, turning once. Roll as directed.

Rich Chocolate Filling

1½ oz. (1½ sq.) unsweetened chocolate
2 tablespoons sugar
1 tablespoon water
⅛ teaspoon salt
2 egg yolks, slightly beaten
½ teaspoon vanilla extract
½ cup butter
1 cup confectioners' sugar

1. Heat chocolate, sugar, water, and salt over boiling water, stirring until mixture is smooth.
2. Blend egg yolks into mixture in double-boiler top and cook 3 to 5 minutes, stirring constantly. Stir in extract; set aside to cool.
3. Cream butter; add confectioners' sugar gradually, beating until fluffy.
4. Add chocolate mixture gradually, beating well; cover and chill.
5. Before using, beat filling with a spoon to soften slightly.

About 1¼ cups

Lacy Almond Crisps

⅓ cup blanched almonds, grated
¼ cup sugar
2 teaspoons flour
3 tablespoons butter or margarine
1 tablespoon milk

1. Mix almonds, sugar, and flour in a bowl. Blend in butter and milk.
2. Drop batter by teaspoonfuls about 4 inches apart onto greased and lightly floured cookie sheets.
3. Bake at 350°F 6 to 7 minutes, or until golden brown.
4. Let set about 1 minute; carefully remove with a spatula to a wire rack. Cool completely. Store in an airtight container.

About 2 dozen 3-inch cookies

Lacy Filbert Crisps: Follow recipe for Lacy Almond Crisps. Substitute ⅓ **cup filberts,** grated, for the almonds. Add ¼ **teaspoon ground mace.**

Almond Macaroons

½ lb. almond paste, cut in pieces
⅓ cup (about 3) egg whites, slightly beaten
¾ teaspoon vanilla extract
1 cup sugar

1. Work almond paste until softened. Add the egg whites gradually, mixing thoroughly.
2. Stir in extract. Add sugar in halves, mixing until blended after each addition.
3. Drop by rounded teaspoonfuls onto cookie sheets lined with unglazed paper (baking parchment or brown).
4. Bake at 300°F about 25 minutes.

About 3 dozen cookies

Pineapple-Raisin Cookies

1 cup firmly packed golden brown sugar
½ cup soft butter or margarine
1 egg
1 teaspoon vanilla extract
½ cup raisins
¾ cup canned crushed pineapple, undrained
2 cups all-purpose flour
1 teaspoon baking powder
½ teaspoon baking soda
½ teaspoon salt
½ cup chopped walnuts (optional)

1. Combine brown sugar, butter, egg, and vanilla extract in mixing bowl. Beat until fluffy.
2. Add raisins and pineapple; mix thoroughly.
3. Combine flour, baking powder, baking soda, and salt; add to the creamed mixture and mix well. Stir in nuts.
4. Drop the mixture by spoonfuls 2 inches apart on greased cookie sheets.
5. Bake at 375°F 12 to 15 minutes.

About 4 dozen cookies

Banana-Bran Cookies

¾ cup sifted all-purpose flour
½ teaspoon baking powder
¼ teaspoon baking soda
¼ teaspoon salt
½ teaspoon ground cinnamon
⅛ teaspoon ground allspice
⅛ teaspoon ground cloves
1 cup bran flakes
½ cup mashed banana
⅓ cup butter
½ cup sugar
1 egg
¼ cup coarsely chopped pecans

1. Sift flour, baking powder, baking soda, salt, and spices together; set aside.
2. Combine bran flakes and the banana; set aside.
3. Cream butter; add sugar gradually, beating until fluffy. Add egg and beat thoroughly.
4. Add dry ingredients to creamed mixture alternately with the banana mixture, mixing until blended after each addition. Stir in pecans.
5. Drop by slightly rounded teaspoonfuls onto greased cookie sheets.
6. Bake at 375°F 10 to 12 minutes.

About 4 dozen cookies

Chocolate Banana-Bran Cookies: Follow recipe for Banana-Bran Cookies. Stir in ½ **cup semisweet chocolate pieces** with the nuts.

Banana Spice Cookies: Follow recipe for Banana-Bran Cookies. Increase flour to ¾ cup plus 2 tablespoons. Decrease cinnamon to ¼ teaspoon. Omit allspice and bran flakes. Substitute **vegetable shortening** for butter. Increase pecans to ½ cup. Drop by tablespoonfuls onto the cookie sheets. If desired, frost cooled cookies with a **Butter Cream Frosting**, *see below,* flavored with a few drops **banana extract.**

Bran Flake Drops: Follow recipe for Banana-Bran Cookies. Increase baking powder to 1 teaspoon; omit baking soda. Omit banana; combine bran flakes with ¼ **cup milk.**

Butter Cream Frosting

½ cup butter
½ teaspoon almond extract
5 cups confectioners' sugar
4 to 5 tablespoons milk or cream

Cream butter with extract. Alternately add confectioners' sugar and milk, beating thoroughly after each addition. Beat until of spreading consistency.

Chocolate Almond Macaroons

1 oz. (1 sq.) unsweetened chocolate
½ lb. almond paste
⅓ cup egg whites, unbeaten (slightly more or less egg white may be needed, depending on moisture in almond paste)
¾ teaspoon vanilla extract
½ cup sugar
½ cup confectioners' sugar

1. Melt the chocolate; set aside to cool.
2. Force almond paste through a coarse sieve a little at a time. Gradually add egg whites, blending until smooth after each addition.
3. Blend in cooled chocolate and the extract.
4. Mix a blend of the sugars, a little at a time, into almond paste mixture; final mixture should be thick enough to hold its shape but must not be stiff.
5. Drop by teaspoonfuls 2 inches apart onto cookie sheets

lined with unglazed paper. Flatten the top of each macaroon.
6. Bake at 300°F 25 to 30 minutes.
7. Remove cookies to wire racks. (If necessary, slightly moisten underside of paper directly under each macaroon to remove.)

About 3 dozen cookies

Yellow Almond Macaroons: Follow recipe for Chocolate Almond Macaroons. Omit chocolate. Mix ¼ **cup sifted flour** with the sugars. Blend ¼ **teaspoon yellow food coloring** with extract. Sift **confectioners' sugar** over tops before baking.

Luscious Chocolate Crispies

- ¾ cup firmly packed light brown sugar
- ¼ cup butter
- 1¼ cups nuts, coarsely chopped
- ½ cup semisweet chocolate pieces
- 1 egg, beaten
- 1 teaspoon vanilla extract
- ¼ teaspoon almond extract

1. Cook brown sugar and butter in a heavy saucepan over low heat 3 minutes, stirring constantly.
2. Remove from heat; stir in nuts and chocolate pieces; cool slightly (about 5 minutes).
3. Add the egg and extracts gradually to chocolate mixture, stirring constantly.
4. Drop by half teaspoonfuls 2 inches apart onto well-greased cookie sheets.
5. Bake at 350°F 8 to 10 minutes.
6. Cool cookies before removing from cookie sheets. (Transfer to wire racks when cookies are "set" but not crisp.)

About 3 dozen cookies

Chocolate-Pecan Kisses

- 2 egg whites
- ⅛ teaspoon salt
- ⅛ teaspoon cream of tartar
- ¾ cup sugar
- 1 teaspoon vanilla extract
- ⅔ cup semisweet chocolate pieces
- ⅔ cup pecans, coarsely chopped

1. Beat the egg whites, salt, and cream of tartar until frothy. Add the sugar gradually, beating until very stiff peaks are formed. Beat in extract.
2. Fold in the chocolate pieces and pecans.
3. Drop by heaping teaspoonfuls 2 inches apart onto cookie sheets covered with unglazed paper (baking parchment or brown).
4. Bake at 300°F 20 to 25 minutes.
5. Remove from paper while still warm.

About 2 dozen cookies

Championship Chocolate Cookies

- 8 oz. (8 sq.) semisweet chocolate
- 2¼ cups sifted all-purpose flour
- 1 teaspoon baking soda
- ½ teaspoon salt
- 1 cup butter
- 2 teaspoons vanilla extract
- 1 cup firmly packed light brown sugar
- ½ cup sugar
- 2 eggs

1. Grate chocolate, preferably using a rotary-type grater with a hand-operated crank.
2. Sift flour, baking soda, and salt together; set aside.
3. Cream butter with extract; add sugars gradually, beating until fluffy. Add eggs, one at a time, beating thoroughly after each addition.
4. Add grated chocolate and dry ingredients in fourths, mixing until blended after each addition.
5. Drop by teaspoonfuls 3 inches apart onto lightly greased cookie sheets.
6. Bake at 350°F about 10 minutes.

About 6 dozen cookies

Walnut Cakes, 64; Walnut Bonnets, 51; Double Swirl Walnut Cookies, 55

Crisp Sugar Cookies

2½ cups sifted all-purpose flour
2 teaspoons cream of tartar
1 teaspoon baking soda
½ teaspoon salt
1 cup butter
1 teaspoon vanilla extract
1 cup sugar
2 eggs

1. Sift flour, cream of tartar, baking soda, and salt together; set aside.
2. Cream butter with extract; add sugar gradually, beating until fluffy. Add eggs, one at a time, beating thoroughly after each addition.
3. Add dry ingredients in fourths, mixing until blended after each addition.
4. Chill dough in refrigerator 1 hour.
5. Shape small balls by dropping small amounts of dough from a teaspoon 2 inches apart onto lightly greased cookie sheets. For glaze (this glaze is very important) dip bottom of a glass in **water;** then dip in **sugar.** Flatten each ball with sugar-coated glass.
6. Bake at 375°F 10 minutes.

About 2 dozen cookies

Imperials

¾ cup unsalted butter
¾ cup sugar
4 egg yolks (about 5 tablespoons), well beaten
1 cup sifted all-purpose flour

1. Cream butter; add sugar gradually, beating until fluffy. Add egg yolks in thirds, beating thoroughly after each addition.
2. Add flour in halves, mixing until blended after each addition. Chill thoroughly, about 2 hours.
3. Using 1½ teaspoons of dough for each cookie, drop dough about 2 inches apart onto ungreased cookie sheets; flatten with a glass dipped in **sugar.**
4. Bake at 350°F about 8 minutes.
5. If desired, dip cooled cookies into **Chocolate Glaze I,** *see below;* place cookies on wire racks until glaze is set.

About 5 dozen cookies

Chocolate Glaze I: Partially melt **3 oz. (½ cup) semi-sweet chocolate pieces** in the top of a double boiler over hot (not simmering) water. Remove from heat and stir until chocolate is melted. Blend in **3 tablespoons butter.**

Double-Chocolate Cherry Drops

2 oz. (2 sq.) unsweetened chocolate
½ cup vegetable shortening
1 teaspoon vanilla extract
1 cup sugar
1 egg
1¼ cups sifted all-purpose flour
1 teaspoon baking powder
1 teaspoon salt
2 tablespoons milk
¾ cup coarsely chopped walnuts
½ cup semisweet chocolate pieces
12 maraschino cherries, coarsely chopped and drained

1. Melt chocolate; set aside to cool.
2. Blend shortening and extract; add sugar gradually, beating until fluffy. Add the egg and beat thoroughly. Blend in cooled chocolate.
3. Sift flour, baking powder, and salt together; add to creamed mixture alternately with milk. Stir in remaining ingredients.
4. Drop by level tablespoons about 2 inches apart onto greased cookie sheets.
5. Bake at 325°F about 10 minutes.
6. Cool slightly; remove cookies to wire racks.

About 4 dozen cookies

Wheat Germ Oatmeal Cookies

⅔ cup butter or margarine, softened
1 teaspoon vanilla extract
1 cup firmly packed brown sugar
½ cup granulated sugar
1 egg
¼ cup milk
1 cup sifted all-purpose flour
¾ teaspoon salt
½ teaspoon baking soda
¾ cup toasted wheat germ
½ cup walnuts, chopped
2½ cups uncooked rolled oats, quick or old-fashioned

1. Put butter, vanilla extract, sugars, egg, and milk into a bowl. Beat thoroughly.
2. Sift flour, salt, and baking soda together; add to creamed mixture and mix well. Stir in wheat germ, walnuts, and oats.
3. Drop by rounded teaspoonfuls onto greased cookie sheets.
4. Bake at 375°F 12 to 15 minutes.

About 6 dozen cookies

Frosted Chocolate Nut Drops

4 oz. (4 sq.) unsweetened chocolate
1 cup butter
2 teaspoons vanilla extract
2 cups sugar
3 eggs
2¾ cups sifted all-purpose flour
½ teaspoon baking powder
½ teaspoon baking soda
½ teaspoon salt
1 cup buttermilk
2 cups black walnuts or walnuts, chopped
Rich Chocolate Frosting, *below*

1. Melt chocolate; set aside to cool.
2. Cream butter with extract; add sugar gradually, beating until fluffy.
3. Add eggs, one at a time, beating thoroughly after each addition. Blend in cooled chocolate.
4. Sift flour, baking powder, baking soda, and salt together; add to creamed mixture alternately with buttermilk, mixing until blended after each addition. Stir in walnuts.
5. Drop by tablespoonfuls about 3 inches apart onto lightly greased cookie sheets.
6. Bake at 350°F 12 to 15 minutes.
7. Spread frosting on cooled cookies.

About 4 dozen cookies

Note: If desired, for 1 cup of nuts substitute 1 cup raisins, 1 cup chopped dates, or ½ cup chopped maraschino cherries.

Rich Chocolate Frosting

½ cup butter or margarine
4 oz. (4 sq.) unsweetened chocolate
2⅔ cups confectioners' sugar
1 egg
6 tablespoons water
2 teaspoons vanilla extract
⅛ teaspoon salt

1. Melt butter and chocolate together. Pour into a bowl. Beat in, in order, the confectioners' sugar, egg, water, extract, and salt.
2. Set bowl in a larger bowl of ice and water. Beat with electric mixer about 5 minutes, or until frosting is of spreading consistency.

Chocolate Meringues

3 egg whites
¾ cup sugar
¾ teaspoon cider vinegar
¾ teaspoon vanilla extract
3 tablespoons Dutch process cocoa

1. Beat egg whites until frothy, using medium speed of electric mixer.
2. Add half of sugar gradually, beating constantly; beat 5 minutes after last addition of sugar.
3. Beat in vinegar and extract. Add remaining sugar gradually, beating constantly. Increase speed to high; beat until very stiff peaks are formed, about 3 minutes. Do not overbeat.
4. Sift cocoa evenly over meringue; using a flexible spatula, carefully fold in the cocoa until almost blended. (Mixture will be streaked.)
5. Force meringue through a pastry bag and star decorating tube, or drop meringue by heaping teaspoonfuls onto cookie sheets covered with unglazed paper; swirl to form rosettes.
6. Bake at 250°F 1½ hours.

About 2 dozen cookies

Mint Meringues: Follow recipe for Chocolate Meringues. Beat **6 drops of red or green food coloring** with egg whites. Omit vanilla extract and cocoa; add ¼ **teaspoon peppermint extract.** Bake at 200°F 1½ hours.

White Meringues: Follow recipe for Chocolate Meringues. Omit cocoa. Bake at 200°F 1½ hours.

Coconut Macaroons

These confectionlike cookies are a crunchy complement to rich vanilla or chocolate ice cream.

⅔ cup (½ of a 14-oz. can) sweetened condensed milk
2 cups flaked coconut
½ to ¾ cup coarsely chopped dry roasted almonds
¼ cup chopped maraschino cherries, drained
1½ teaspoons vanilla extract

1. Mix all ingredients thoroughly. Drop by rounded teaspoonfuls onto well-greased cookie sheet. To speed removal of cookies from cookie sheet, bake no more than 12 at a time.
2. Bake at 350°F 10 to 12 minutes, or until delicately browned.
3. Immediately loosen all cookies from cookie sheet and remove cookies to wire rack at once.

About 3 dozen cookies

Note: For filling small tart shells, blend remaining ½ can of sweetened condensed milk with ⅓ **cup lemon juice** and 1 or more drops **yellow food coloring;** stir just until mixture thickens. Fill; garnish with whipped topping.

Coconut Macaroons DeLuxe

7 oz. flaked coconut, finely chopped (in blender, if desired); about 2½ cups, chopped
¾ cup (about 6) egg whites, unbeaten
1 cup sugar

1. Put all ingredients into a 2-quart saucepan and mix thoroughly. Set over very low heat and stir until mixture is thickened and sugar is dissolved, about 20 minutes; keep temperature of mixture just below 150°F.
2. Remove from heat; cool 5 minutes.
3. Force through pastry bag and No. 7 star tube, which has

1 tablespoon cornstarch
¼ teaspoon almond extract

been opened entirely, or drop by heaping teaspoonfuls directly onto cookie sheets lined with unglazed paper.
4. Press a **candied cherry piece** onto top of each.
5. Bake at 350°F 20 minutes.
6. Remove cookies to wire racks. (If necessary, slightly moisten underside of paper directly under each macaroon to remove.)

About 3 dozen cookies

Chocolate Macaroons: Follow recipe for Coconut Macaroons de Luxe. Add **2 ounces (2 squares) unsweetened chocolate,** grated, to saucepan with coconut. Heat mixture to 120°F about 5 minutes.

Brandy Snaps

¾ cup plus 2 tablespoons sifted
      all-purpose flour
½ cup sugar
1 teaspoon ground ginger
6 tablespoons butter
¼ cup light corn syrup
2 tablespoons brandy
1 teaspoon grated lemon peel
1 tablespoon lemon juice

1. Put a cookie sheet into the oven while oven is preheating.
2. Sift flour, sugar, and ginger together; set aside.
3. Heat the butter and corn syrup together over low heat just until butter is melted; stir to blend.
4. Remove from heat. Add dry ingredients in halves to butter-syrup mixture, mixing until well blended after each addition. Blend in the remaining ingredients. Beat until thick and creamy.
5. Remove hot cookie sheet from oven and quickly grease it. Drop batter by half teaspoonfuls about 4 inches apart onto the cookie sheets. (Bake only 3 or 4 cookies at one time; they are difficult to remove when cooled.) Spread each cookie evenly with a spatula.
6. Bake at 400°F 4 to 5 minutes, or until golden brown and lacy.
7. Remove cookie sheet to wire rack. Cool 1 to 2 minutes. As soon as the cookies can be lifted, remove and roll, lacy side out, around greased wooden spoon handles. Cool on rack.

About 4½ dozen cookies

Tipsy Currant Chasers

½ cup unsalted butter
½ cup sugar
2 eggs
1 cup sifted all-purpose flour
   Currants in Rum, *below*

1. Cream butter; add sugar gradually, beating until fluffy. Add eggs, one at a time, beating thoroughly after each addition.
2. Add flour, ½ cup at a time, mixing until blended after each addition.
3. Stir in 1 cup of drained currants; let stand 10 to 15 minutes to allow flavors to blend.
4. Drop by teaspoonfuls 2 inches apart onto lightly greased cookie sheets.
5. Bake at 425°F 6 minutes.

About 4 dozen cookies

Currants in Rum: Combine **2 cups currants** and **1 cup rum** in a jar; cover tightly and store in refrigerator. Shake occasionally. The longer currants are stored, the more flavor will be absorbed. Remaining currants may be stored for use in other food preparation, adding more currants as needed.

Virginia Rebels

1 cup sifted all-purpose flour
½ teaspoon baking soda
½ teaspoon salt
6 tablespoons cocoa
1¼ cups butter
1 teaspoon vanilla extract
1½ cups sugar
1 egg
¼ cup water
3 cups uncooked rolled oats

1. Sift flour, baking soda, salt, and cocoa together; set aside.
2. Cream butter with extract; add sugar gradually, beating until fluffy. Add the egg and beat well.
3. Alternately add dry ingredients with water, mixing until blended after each addition. Add rolled oats gradually, stirring well.
4. Drop by teaspoonfuls 2 inches apart onto ungreased cookie sheets.
5. Bake at 350°F about 12 minutes.

About 15 dozen cookies

Note: If desired, after addition of rolled oats, mix in any of the following: **1 cup chopped dark seedless raisins, 6 ounces semisweet chocolate pieces, 1 cup drained, chopped maraschino cherries,** or **½ cup chopped candied cherries and ½ cup chopped candied pineapple.**

Soft Ginger Creams

2 cups sifted all-purpose flour
½ teaspoon baking soda
¼ teaspoon salt
2 teaspoons ground ginger
¼ teaspoon ground cinnamon
¾ cup butter or margarine
1 cup firmly packed light brown sugar
3 tablespoons light molasses
1 egg
½ cup dairy sour cream
Glossy Orange Frosting, *below*

1. Sift the flour, baking soda, salt, and spices together; set aside.
2. Cream butter with brown sugar; blend in molasses. Add egg and beat well.
3. Mixing until blended after each addition, add dry ingredients in thirds and sour cream in halves.
4. Drop by teaspoonfuls about 2 inches apart onto lightly greased cookie sheets.
5. Bake at 375°F 8 to 10 minutes.
6. Remove cookies to wire racks to cool. Frost with Glossy Orange Frosting.

7 dozen cookies

Glossy Orange Frosting: Beat **1 egg white** slightly. Blend in **1½ cups confectioners' sugar.** Add **1 tablespoon butter,** melted, **⅛ teaspoon salt, 1 teaspoon vanilla extract,** and **1 teaspoon orange extract;** beat until smooth.

About 1 cup

Mount Shasta Cookies

Each cookie is baked with a mounded topping of coconut meringue, reminding one of a Western mountain peak.

½ cup shortening
1 teaspoon vanilla extract
½ cup sugar
½ cup firmly packed brown sugar
1 egg yolk
1½ cups sifted all-purpose flour
¾ teaspoon salt
3 tablespoons milk
1 cup walnuts, chopped

1. Cream shortening with extract; add ½ cup sugar and brown sugar gradually, beating until fluffy. Add egg yolk; beat thoroughly.
2. Blend flour and salt; add to creamed mixture alternately with milk, mixing until blended after each addition. Stir in walnuts.
3. Drop by rounded teaspoonfuls onto ungreased cookie sheets; flatten slightly. Set aside.
4. Beat egg white until frothy; add ½ cup sugar gradually,

1 egg white
½ cup sugar
1 cup flaked coconut

beating constantly until stiff peaks are formed. Blend in coconut.
5. Top each cookie round with a teaspoonful of coconut meringue, shaping into a peak.
6. Bake at 375°F 10 to 12 minutes.

About 4½ dozen cookies

Stouffer's Oatmeal Macaroons

From the famous Stouffer Restaurant chain.

½ cup butter
1 cup quick-cooking rolled oats
½ cup plus 2 tablespoons sugar
¼ cup cake flour
½ teaspoon baking powder
¼ teaspoon salt
1 egg, slightly beaten
½ teaspoon vanilla extract
¼ cup chopped nuts

1. Melt butter in a 2-quart saucepan. Stir in rolled oats and brown lightly over medium heat (3 to 4 minutes), stirring constantly; set aside to cool.
2. Blend sugar, flour, baking powder, and salt; stir into cooled oats.
3. Blend in egg and extract; beat thoroughly. Stir in nuts.
4. Drop by rounded teaspoonfuls 3 inches apart onto lightly greased cookie sheets.
5. Bake at 360°F 10 to 12 minutes.
6. While still hot, transfer to wire rack.

About 2 dozen cookies

Frosted Apricot Nut Drops

1 cup sifted all-purpose flour
¼ cup sugar
1½ teaspoons baking powder
½ cup butter or margarine
3 oz. cream cheese, softened
½ teaspoon vanilla extract
½ cup apricot preserves
½ cup chopped pecans
Apricot Frosting, *below*

1. Sift flour, sugar, and baking powder together; set aside.
2. Cream butter with cream cheese and extract thoroughly. Beat in apricot preserves until blended. Add dry ingredients and mix until blended. Stir in pecans.
3. Drop mixture by teaspoonfuls onto ungreased cookie sheets.
4. Bake at 350°F about 12 minutes, or until edges are delicately browned.
5. Spread Apricot Frosting on top of cooled cookies, or spread on bottom and sandwich two cookies together.

About 4 dozen cookies

Apricot Frosting: Blend **2 tablespoons butter or margarine** and **1 cup apricot preserves** with **1 cup confectioners' sugar** until well mixed.

Orange Oatmeal Cookies

1¾ cups sifted all-purpose flour
4 teaspoons baking powder
1 teaspoon salt
1 teaspoon ground nutmeg
1¼ cups butter or margarine
¼ cup grated orange peel
2 cups sugar
1 egg
2 cups uncooked rolled oats

1. Sift flour, baking powder, salt, and nutmeg together; set aside.
2. Cream butter with orange peel; add the sugar gradually, beating until fluffy. Add the egg and beat thoroughly.
3. Add dry ingredients in thirds, mixing until blended after each addition. Stir in the rolled oats.
4. Drop by teaspoonfuls 3 inches apart onto lightly greased cookie sheets.
5. Bake at 375°F 12 to 15 minutes.

About 6 dozen cookies

Note: For a more nutritious and an equally delicious cookie, increase the rolled oats to 3 cups.

Plantation Crisps

¼ cup butter
½ teaspoon vanilla extract
1 cup firmly packed dark brown
  sugar
1 egg
½ cup sifted all-purpose flour
¼ teaspoon salt
1 cup pecans, coarsely chopped

1. Cream butter with extract; add brown sugar gradually, beating until fluffy. Add egg and beat thoroughly.
2. Blend flour and salt; add to creamed mixture in halves, mixing until blended after each addition. Stir in the pecans.
3. Drop by teaspoonfuls 3 inches apart onto ungreased cookie sheets; bake about 6 cookies at one time (they are difficult to remove when cooled).
4. Bake at 350°F 10 to 12 minutes.
5. Immediately remove cookies to wire racks to cool.

About 3½ dozen cookies

Pumpkin Jumbos

2 cups dark seedless raisins
1½ cups water
4½ cups sifted all-purpose flour
1 teaspoon baking powder
1 teaspoon baking soda
1 teaspoon salt
1¼ cups butter or margarine
1 teaspoon ground cinnamon
¼ teaspoon ground allspice
¼ teaspoon ground nutmeg
1 teaspoon vanilla extract
2 cups sugar
3 eggs
1 cup chopped walnuts
  Creamy Orange Frosting

1. Combine raisins and water in a saucepan. Bring to boiling and simmer 5 minutes. Drain, reserving ½ cup liquid. Set raisins and liquid aside.
2. Sift flour, baking powder, baking soda, and salt together; set aside.
3. Cream butter with spices and extract; add sugar gradually, beating until fluffy. Add eggs, one at a time, beating thoroughly after each addition.
4. Add dry ingredients alternately with raisin liquid, mixing until blended after each addition. Mix in raisins and walnuts.
5. Drop by heaping tablespoonfuls 2 inches apart onto lightly greased cookie sheets.
6. Bake at 400°F about 10 minutes.
7. Remove to wire racks. When cool, frost with Creamy Orange Frosting. Decorate to resemble jack-o'-lantern faces. With a wooden pick or fine brush dipped in **melted chocolate,**

draw lines to indicate grooves in pumpkin and to make the face. Use a piece of **citron** or **angelica** for stem.

About 4 dozen cookies

Creamy Orange Frosting

- ¼ cup butter or margarine
- 1½ teaspoons vanilla extract
- ⅛ teaspoon salt
- 1 lb. (about 3½ cups) confectioners' sugar
- 1 egg yolk
- 2 to 3 tablespoons orange juice
  Red and yellow food coloring

1. Cream the butter with extract and salt. Add the confectioners' sugar gradually, creaming until blended. Add egg yolk and beat until smooth.
2. Add the orange juice gradually, beating until frosting is of desired consistency. Blend in food coloring, one drop at a time (approximately 3 drops of red and 6 drops of yellow), until frosting is tinted a light orange.

About 1⅓ cups

Queen Bees

- ½ cup butter
- ½ cup sugar
- ½ cup honey
- 1 egg
- 1¾ cups sifted all-purpose flour
- 1 teaspoon baking powder
- ½ teaspoon salt
- ¼ cup sherry
- 1 cup chopped toasted blanched almonds
- ½ cup finely chopped crystallized ginger

1. Cream butter; add sugar gradually, then honey, creaming until fluffy. Add egg and beat thoroughly.
2. Sift flour, baking powder, and salt together; add to creamed mixture alternately with sherry, mixing until blended after each addition. Stir in a mixture of almonds and ginger.
3. Chill dough thoroughly.
4. Drop by teaspoonfuls 2 inches apart onto lightly greased cookie sheets.
5. Bake at 400°F about 10 minutes.

About 4½ dozen cookies

Chocolate Bees: Follow recipe for Queen Bees. Omit crystallized ginger; use ½ **cup finely chopped chocolate-coated crystallized ginger.**

Nut Colonels

- 1 egg
- ½ cup sugar
- ¼ teaspoon vanilla extract
- 1½ cups salted peanuts or cashews, coarsely chopped
- 2 teaspoons flour

1. Beat egg, sugar, and extract until thick. Add nuts and flour gradually, folding in after each addition.
2. Drop by teaspoonfuls 2 inches apart onto greased cookie sheets.
3. Bake at 350°F 10 to 12 minutes.

About 3 dozen cookies

Symphonies

A delectable blend, a veritable symphony of flavors, each a counterpoint to delicious applesauce.

¾ cup butter
1½ teaspoons vanilla extract
 1 teaspoon grated lemon peel
¾ cup granulated sugar or firmly
   packed brown sugar
 1 egg
1¾ cups sifted all-purpose flour
½ teaspoon baking soda
¼ teaspoon salt
⅓ cup thick applesauce

1. Cream butter with extract and lemon peel; add brown sugar gradully, beating until fluffy. Add the egg and beat thoroughly.
2. Sift flour, baking soda, and salt together; add to creamed mixture alternately with applesauce, mixing until blended after each addition.
3. Drop by teaspoonfuls 2 inches apart onto ungreased cookie sheets.
4. Bake at 400°F 6 to 8 minutes.

About 6 dozen cookies

Spiced Symphonies: Follow recipe for Symphonies. Blend with dry ingredients the following ground spices: ½ **teaspoon cinnamon, ¼ teaspoon nutmeg, ¼ teaspoon mace,** and ⅛ **teaspoon cloves;** or **1 teaspoon cinnamon;** or **1 teaspoon nutmeg.**

Raisin Symphonies: Follow recipe for Symphonies. After addition of dry ingredients, mix in **1 cup dark seedless raisins** and ½ **cup chopped walnuts.**

Apple Butter Symphonies: Follow recipe for Symphonies. Omit lemon peel; substitute **6 tablespoons apple butter** for the applesauce.

Chocolate Symphonies: Follow recipe for Symphonies. Omit lemon peel; after addition of egg, blend in **2 ounces (2 squares) unsweetened chocolate,** melted and cooled.

Brazil Nut Cookies

½ cup butter
¾ teaspoon vanilla extract
¼ teaspoon almond extract
 2 tablespoons honey
 1 cup sifted all-purpose flour
⅛ teaspoon salt
¾ cup Brazil nuts, finely chopped

1. Cream butter with extracts; beat in the honey.
2. Mix flour and salt; add ½ cup at a time to creamed mixture, mixing until blended after each addition; stir in nuts.
3. Drop by teaspoonfuls about 2 inches apart onto ungreased cookie sheets.
4. Bake at 350°F 12 to 15 minutes.
5. Cool 2 to 3 minutes before removing cookies to wire racks. Immediately sift Vanilla Confectioners' Sugar, *page 59,* over cookies; cool completely.

About 3 dozen cookies

Maple Pecan Drops: Follow recipe for Brazil Nut Cookies. Omit Brazil nuts; use ¾ **cup finely chopped pecans.** Omit honey; use ¼ **cup firmly packed maple sugar.** (If maple sugar is available only in solid form, grate before using; or heat over simmering water until sugar is softened, then force through a fine sieve).

Peanut Bounties

One recipe of these marvelous crispy cookies will easily fill several cookie jars.

1 cup butter
1 cup firmly packed brown sugar
1 egg
1 cup sifted all-purpose flour
½ teaspoon baking powder
½ teaspoon baking soda
½ cup crushed corn flakes
1 cup uncooked rolled oats
¾ cup to 1 cup salted Spanish
    peanuts

1. Cream butter; add brown sugar gradually, beating until fluffy. Add the egg and beat thoroughly.
2. Sift flour, baking powder, and baking soda together; add to creamed mixture in halves, mixing until blended after each addition. Stir in the remaining ingredients.
3. Drop by half-teaspoonfuls 2 inches apart onto ungreased cookie sheets.
4. Bake at 375°F 5 to 7 minutes.
5. Remove cookie sheets to wire racks; cool about 3 minutes before removing cookies.

About 14 dozen cookies

Peanut Butter Bounties: Follow recipe for Peanut Bounties. Decrease butter to ¾ cup; cream with ¼ **cup peanut butter** and **1 teaspoon vanilla extract.** Substitute **granulated sugar** for brown sugar. Increase eggs to 2 and flour to 1⅔ cups; omit corn flakes and rolled oats.

Temple Bells

1½ cups sifted all-purpose flour
½ teaspoon baking soda
⅛ teaspoon salt
1½ teaspoons instant coffee
½ teaspoon ground mace
¼ teaspoon ground cinnamon
¼ teaspoon ground nutmeg
¾ cup butter
1 cup firmly packed brown sugar
1 egg
1 cup dark seedless raisins
½ cup nuts, coarsely chopped

1. Sift flour, baking soda, salt, coffee, and spices together; set aside.
2. Cream butter; add brown sugar gradually, beating until fluffy. Add egg and beat thoroughly.
3. Add dry ingredients in thirds, mixing until blended after each addition. Stir in raisins and nuts.
4. Drop by teaspoonfuls 2 inches apart onto lightly greased cookie sheets.
5. Bake at 375°F 8 to 10 minutes.

About 5 dozen cookies

Chocolate-Pecan Delights

2½ cups pecans, grated
2 oz. (2 sq.) unsweetened chocolate,
    grated
2 cups sifted Vanilla Confectioners'
    Sugar, *Page 59*
4 egg whites
⅛ teaspoon salt

1. Combine pecans, chocolate, and confectioners' sugar; mix thoroughly.
2. Beat egg whites and salt until stiff peaks are formed; gently fold in the nut-sugar mixture in small amounts.
3. Drop by teaspoonfuls about 2 inches apart onto greased cookie sheets.
4. Bake at 350°F 10 to 12 minutes.
5. Immediately remove cookies to wire racks.

About 8 dozen cookies

Orange Candy Crisps

⅔ cup sifted all-purpose flour
½ teaspoon baking powder
¼ teaspoon baking soda
⅛ teaspoon salt
½ lb. (about 1¼ cups) jellied candy
 orange slices, cut in small pieces
3 tablespoons flour
¾ cup butter or margarine
½ teaspoon vanilla extract
½ cup sugar
½ cup firmly packed brown sugar
1 egg
¾ cup uncooked rolled oats
½ cup flaked coconut

1. Sift ⅔ cup flour, baking powder, baking soda, and salt together; set aside.
2. Mix candy orange pieces with the 3 tablespoons flour; set aside.
3. Cream butter with extract; add the sugars gradually, beating until fluffy. Add the egg and beat thoroughly.
4. Add dry ingredients in halves, mixing until blended after each addition. Stir in the candy orange pieces, rolled oats, and coconut.
5. Drop by teaspoonfuls 2 inches apart onto greased cookie sheets.
6. Bake at 375°F 10 to 12 minutes.
7. If necessary, cool cookies slightly before transferring to wire racks.

About 7 dozen cookies

Gingersnaps

3 cups sifted all-purpose flour
3 teaspoons baking soda
3 teaspoons ground ginger
½ teaspoon ground cinnamon
1 cup butter
1 sugar
½ cup molasses
1 egg

1. Sift flour, baking soda, ginger, and cinnamon together; set aside.
2. Cream butter; add sugar gradually, beating until fluffy. Blend in molasses. Add egg and beat thoroughly.
3. Add dry ingredients in thirds, mixing until blended after each addition.
4. Drop by teaspoonfuls about 3 inches apart onto ungreased cookie sheets; sprinkle generously with **sugar.**
5. Bake at 350°F 10 to 12 minutes.

About 6 dozen cookies

Date Drops

1¼ cups sifted all-purpose flour
½ teaspoon baking soda
¼ teaspoon baking powder
¼ teaspoon salt
½ cup butter
½ teaspoon vanilla extract
¾ cup firmly packed brown sugar
1 egg
¼ cup dairy sour cream
7 oz. pitted dates, chopped (about 1 cup)
¼ cup walnuts, chopped
 Frosting, *below*

1. Sift flour, baking soda, baking powder, and salt together; set aside.
2. Cream butter with extract; gradually add brown sugar, beating until fluffy. Add the egg and beat thoroughly.
3. Alternately add dry ingredients in thirds and sour cream in halves, mixing until blended after each addition. Mix in dates and walnuts.
4. Drop by teaspoonfuls about 2 inches apart onto greased cookie sheets.
5. Bake at 375°F 10 minutes.
6. Remove cookies to wire racks to cool completely. Spread Frosting over cookies.

About 4 dozen cookies

Frosting: Heat ¼ **cup butter** in a saucepan until golden brown. Remove from heat. Add **1 cup confectioners' sugar** gradually, beating well after each addition. Blend in ½ **teaspoon vanilla extract** and **5 teaspoons hot water;** beat until frosting is of spreading consistency.

Molded, Pressed, and Refrigerator Cookies

Cookie baking benefits from a little artistry; that's one reason it's so satisfying. We can't all be Picasso, but each of us can add our own personal flourish to cookies. With just a little practice, we can transform a lump of dough into as many shapes as there are snowflakes. And if your family is like most, they will last about as long. ¶ Among the most popular ways of shaping cookies are molding, refrigerating and slicing, and pushing through a cookie press.

For molded cookies, you start with a dough that is quite stiff. Shaping is easier if the dough is chilled a little first, and if you work with hands that you've rubbed with flour. Pinch off a piece of dough and roll it between your palms to form a ball, log, or crescent.

For some molded cookies, the dough balls are flattened with a thumbprint, to be filled after baking with jelly or a tinted icing. Peanut butter cookies are often flattened with the tines of a fork to make a crisscross pattern. Another way is to use the bottom of a glass which has been greased, then dipped in flour or granulated sugar. Redip before each use. If you are the lucky owner of a pretty tumbler with a cut-glass bottom, it can be used to good effect.

If your molded cookies call for a confectioners' sugar coating after baking, coat once while the cookies are still warm, and again after they are room temperature.

Refrigerator cookies are much like molded cookies, but rather than having to shape each one individually, you roll a hefty chunk of dough into a long roll, then chill. Before baking, simply slice crosswise, and cookies are formed.

Pressed cookies—the ones you put through a cylinder equipped with a decorative tip—are made from a buttery-rich batter (margarine usually works as well and helps the budget).

Some bakers like to form the dough into rolls just as for refrigerator cookies, making the rolls the same diameter as the cookie press, then chilling. Refrigerated dough holds its shape better during baking. When you are ready to bake, cut off a length to fit the press, and slip it inside.

Not all cookie presses are alike, so you'll need to follow the directions that come with yours. For many types, it helps to judge how big you want the cookie, then "back off" shortly before enough dough appears. The rest will follow as you lift the press. For strips, a knife to cut them helps.

Pressed cookies have almost become typecast as holiday cookies, and too often the press sits on the shelf from one December to the next. That's unfortunate, as pressing gives the maximum number of cookies for a minimum of effort. And they add a party touch to an otherwise ordinary day.

Almond Cakes

½ cup unsalted butter
1 tablespoon dry gin
¼ teaspoon almond extract
¼ cup sugar
1 cup sifted all-purpose flour
¼ teaspoon baking powder
2 tablespoons finely chopped toasted blanched almonds
Blanched almond halves

1. Cream butter with gin and extract; add sugar gradually, beating until fluffy.
2. Sift flour and baking powder together; add, ½ cup at a time, to creamed mixture, mixing until blended after each addition. Mix in chopped almonds.
3. Using 1 teaspoon dough at a time, shape into balls and place on lightly floured cookie sheets. Flatten each until about ¼ inch thick and press an almond half onto each.
4. Bake at 350°F 12 to 15 minutes.

About 3 dozen cookies

Sugared Cocoa Delights

1¼ cups butter
1 teaspoon vanilla extract
1 cup confectioners' sugar
2 cups sifted all-purpose flour
½ cup unsweetened cocoa
¼ teaspoon salt
1 cup chopped pecans
Confectioners' sugar for coating

1. Cream butter with vanilla extract. Add confectioners' sugar gradually, creaming well.
2. Blend flour, cocoa, and salt; add to creamed mixture and mix well. Stir in pecans.
3. Pinch off small amounts of dough and place on ungreased cookie sheets.
4. Bake at 350°F about 15 minutes. Cool on wire racks. Coat with confectioners' sugar.

About 8 dozen cookies

Moji Pearls

¾ cup butter
½ teaspoon vanilla extract
⅓ cup sugar
1½ cups sifted all-purpose flour
⅛ teaspoon salt

1. Cream butter with extract; add sugar gradually, beating until fluffy.
2. Blend flour and salt; add in thirds to creamed mixture, mixing until blended after each addition. Chill dough until easy to handle.
3. Shape into 1-inch balls or into crescents (if desired, roll in sesame seed). Place about 2 inches apart on ungreased cookie sheets.
4. Bake at 325°F 20 minutes.

About 3 dozen cookies

Pecan Poofs: Follow recipe for Moji Pearls. Substitute ¼ **cup confectioners' sugar** for sugar. Decrease flour to 1 cup. Mix in **1 cup pecans**, finely chopped. Shape dough into balls or pyramids.

Citrus Pearls: Follow recipe for Moji Pearls. Substitute **1 tablespoon grated lemon** or **orange peel** for extract.

Spicy Ginger Crunchies

2¼ cups sifted all-purpose flour
2 teaspoons baking soda
1 teaspoon salt
1 teaspoon ground cinnamon
¾ teaspoon ground ginger
½ teaspoon ground cloves
¾ cup butter
1 teaspoon vanilla extract
1 cup sugar
1 egg
¼ cup molasses

1. Sift flour, baking soda, salt, and spices together; set aside.
2. Cream butter with extract; gradually add sugar, beating until light and fluffy. Add egg and molasses; beat thoroughly.
3. Gradually add dry ingredients to creamed mixture, mixing until blended. Chill several hours.
4. Shape dough into ¾-inch balls, roll in **sugar** and place 2 inches apart on greased cookie sheets.
5. Bake at 375°F 7 to 8 minutes.
6. Immediately remove to wire racks to cool.

6 to 7 dozen cookies

Cherry Jewels

½ cup butter
1 teaspoon vanilla extract
¼ cup sugar
1 egg
1 teaspoon grated lemon peel
1 tablespoon lemon juice
1¼ cups sifted all-purpose flour
¾ cup finely chopped pecans
18 candied cherries, halved

1. Cream butter with extract and sugar until light and fluffy. Add the egg and lemon peel and juice; beat thoroughly. Gradually add flour, mixing until blended. Chill.
2. Shape dough into 1-inch balls, roll in chopped pecans and place on greased cookie sheets. Press a cherry half onto center of each ball.
3. Bake at 350°F 10 to 12 minutes.
4. Cool on wire racks.

3 dozen cookies

Princess Gems

¾ cup butter
1 cup sugar
1¼ cups sifted all-purpose flour
1 teaspoon crushed ammonium carbonate (available at your pharmacy)
½ cup flaked coconut

1. Cream butter; add sugar gradually, beating until fluffy.
2. Blend flour and ammonium carbonate; add in halves to creamed mixture, mixing until blended after each addition. Mix in coconut.
3. Shape dough into ¾-inch balls; place 2 inches apart on ungreased cookie sheet.
4. Bake at 325°F about 12 minutes.
5. Cool cookies slightly; sift **confectioners' sugar** over them.

About 5½ dozen cookies

Gumdrop Gems

1 cup vegetable shortening
¾ teaspoon vanilla extract
½ cup granulated sugar
½ cup firmly packed brown sugar
2 eggs, beaten
2 cups sifted all-purpose flour
½ teaspoon baking soda
½ teaspoon salt
1½ cups uncooked rolled oats, quick or old-fashioned
48 small gumdrops

1. Cream shortening with vanilla extract. Add sugars gradually, creaming well. Add eggs and beat thoroughly.
2. Sift flour, baking soda, and salt together; add to creamed mixture and mix well. Stir in oats.
3. Shape dough into balls and put on greased cookie sheets. Make a hollow in each ball and place a gumdrop in each hollow.
4. Bake at 375°F 10 to 12 minutes.

4 dozen cookies

Snowball Meltaways

1 cup butter
½ cup confectioners' sugar
1 teaspoon vanilla extract
2½ cups sifted all-purpose flour
½ cup finely chopped pecans

1. In a heavy saucepan over low heat, melt and heat butter until light brown in color. Pour into a small mixing bowl; chill until firm.
2. Cream browned butter with confectioners' sugar and extract until light and fluffy. Gradually add flour, mixing until blended. Stir in the pecans. Chill several hours for ease in handling.
3. Shape into 1-inch balls. Place on ungreased cookie sheets.
4. Bake at 350°F about 20 minutes.
5. Remove to wire racks. While still hot, dust with **confectioners' sugar.**

About 4 dozen cookies

Coffee-Walnut Fingers

½ cup butter or margarine
¾ cup firmly packed brown sugar
¼ cup heavy cream
2 cups sifted all-purpose flour
½ teaspoon baking powder
½ teaspoon salt
2 teaspoons instant coffee
Frosting, *below*
½ cup chopped walnuts

1. Cream butter; add brown sugar gradually, beating until fluffy. Mix in cream.
2. Sift flour, baking powder, salt, and instant coffee together; add in thirds to creamed mixture, mixing until blended after each addition.
3. Chill dough several hours.
4. Shape dough into "fingers" about 2 inches long and ¼ inch diameter. Place on ungreased cookie sheets.
5. Bake at 350°F 7 minutes.
6. Remove to wire racks. Dip one end of each cooled cookie into Frosting, then into walnuts. Sift **confectioners' sugar** over unfrosted portion of cookies. Place cookies on rack until chocolate is set.

About 8 dozen cookies

Frosting: Combine ½ **cup semisweet chocolate pieces, 2 tablespoons sugar,** and **2 tablespoons water** in the top of a double boiler. Set over hot water until chocolate is melted. Remove from water; stir in ½ **teaspoon vanilla extract.**

Ginger Cookies

2 cups sifted all-purpose flour
1 teaspoon baking powder
½ teaspoon baking soda
½ teaspoon salt
1 teaspoon ground cinnamon
1 teaspoon ground ginger
½ teaspoon ground cloves
½ teaspoon ground mace
1 cup butter
1 cup firmly packed brown sugar
¼ cup dark molasses
1 egg

1. Sift flour, baking powder, baking soda, salt, and spices together; set aside.
2. Cream butter; add brown sugar gradually, beating until fluffy. Blend in molasses. Add egg and beat thoroughly.
3. Add dry ingredients in fourths, mixing until blended after each addition. Chill thoroughly.
4. Shape dough into 1-inch balls and dip in **sugar.** Place 2 inches apart on ungreased cookie sheets.
5. Bake at 350°F 10 to 15 minutes.

About 6 dozen cookies

Anise Cookie Sticks

½ cup butter
3 oz. cream cheese
1 cup sugar
4 eggs
3¼ cups sifted all-purpose flour
3 teaspoons baking powder
½ teaspoon salt
2 teaspoons anise seed

1. Cream butter and cream cheese together. Add sugar gradually, beating thoroughly after each addition. Beat in eggs one at a time; continue beating until light and fluffy.
2. Add a mixture of the remaining ingredients; mix well.
3. Divide dough in half, place on a lightly greased cookie sheet, and form into 2 rolls the length of baking sheet and 1½ inches wide.
4. Bake at 350°F 30 to 35 minutes, or until light brown.
5. Remove from oven and cut rolls crosswise into slices about ¾ inch thick. Place on cookie sheets cut side down. Return to oven. Bake 10 minutes, or until toasted and crisp.

About 4 dozen cookies

Lumberjack Cookies

2 cups sifted all-purpose flour
½ teaspoon baking soda
½ teaspoon salt
1 teaspoon ground cinnamon
1 teaspoon ground ginger
⅔ cup butter
½ cup sugar
½ cup dark molasses
1 egg

1. Sift flour, baking soda, salt, cinnamon, and ginger together; set aside.
2. Cream butter; add sugar gradually, beating until fluffy. Add molasses gradually, blending well. Add egg and beat thoroughly.
3. Add dry ingredients in fourths, mixing until blended. Chill the dough thoroughly.
4. Shape dough into 1-inch balls; roll in **sugar;** place 2 inches apart on ungreased cookie sheets.
5. Bake at 350°F 10 to 12 minutes.

About 4 dozen cookies

Lumberjack Thins: Follow recipe for Lumberjack Cookies. Increase butter to 1¼ cups. Use light for dark molasses. Shape into ¾-inch balls.

Buttery Crunch Cookies

¾ cup butter
1 teaspoon almond extract
¾ cup sugar
1 egg
1½ cups sifted all-purpose flour
½ teaspoon baking powder
½ cup grapenuts
½ cup uncooked rolled oats

1. Cream butter with extract; add sugar gradually, beating until fluffy. Add egg and beat thoroughly.
2. Sift flour and baking powder together; add in thirds to creamed mixture, mixing until blended after each addition. Stir in the cereals.
3. Chill the dough until easy to handle.
4. Shape into 1-inch balls; place about 2 inches apart on ungreased cookie sheets. Dip the bottom of a glass in **sugar** and press each ball to flatten slightly, then with a fork form a crisscross pattern on the tops.
5. Bake at 375°F 8 to 10 minutes.

About 5½ dozen cookies

Lemon Angels

Red, yellow, and green food
    coloring
1¾ cups flaked coconut
1 cup butter
1 teaspoon vanilla extract
1½ cups sifted confectioners' sugar
1 egg
2¼ cups all-purpose flour
½ teaspoon baking soda
¼ teaspoon salt
1 tablespoon grated lemon peel

1. To tint coconut, use 3 jars, one for each color. Blend 2 or 3 drops food coloring with a few drops of water in each jar. Put one-third of coconut into each jar; cover and shake vigorously until coconut is evenly tinted. Turn into shallow dishes and set aside.
2. Cream butter with vanilla extract in a bowl. Add confectioners' sugar gradually, creaming well. Add egg and beat thoroughly.
3. Blend flour, baking soda, and salt; add gradually to creamed mixture, mixing well. Stir in lemon peel.
4. Divide dough into thirds and chill until easy to handle.
5. For each third, roll teaspoonfuls of dough in one color of coconut, form balls, and place on ungreased cookie sheets.
6. Bake at 325°F 10 to 12 minutes. Remove immediately to wire racks to cool.

About 8 dozen cookies

Peanut Butter Cookies

½ cup shortening (half butter)
½ cup peanut butter
½ cup sugar
½ cup firmly packed brown sugar
1 extra-large egg
1¼ cups sifted all-purpose flour
¾ teaspoon baking soda
½ teaspoon baking powder
¼ teaspoon salt

1. Cream shortening and peanut butter until blended; add sugars gradually, beating until fluffy.
2. Add egg and beat thoroughly.
3. Sift remaining ingredients together; add in halves to creamed mixture, mixing until blended after each addition.
4. Shape dough into 1¼-inch balls; place 3 inches apart on lightly greased cookie sheets. Flatten with fork, making a crisscross pattern on the tops.
5. Bake at 375°F about 10 minutes.

About 3 dozen cookies

Note: For a pleasing variation, add snipped **raisins** to the cookie dough before shaping into balls.

Butter Pecan Cookies

1 cup butter
1½ teaspoons vanilla extract
½ teaspoon almond extract
1 cup confectioners' sugar
2 cups sifted all-purpose flour
¼ teaspoon salt
2 egg yolks, slightly beaten
1 tablespoon cream
½ cup pecan halves

1. Cream butter with extracts; add confectioners' sugar gradually, beating until fluffy.
2. Blend the flour and salt; add in fourths to creamed mixture, mixing only until blended after each addition.
3. Shape dough into 1-inch balls. Place about 2 inches apart on ungreased cookie sheets. Flatten each ball to form a cookie round.
4. Blend egg yolks with cream and brush lightly over tops of cookies. Press pecan half onto center of each.
5. Bake at 400°F 10 to 12 minutes, or until very lightly browned.
6. Immediately remove cookies to wire racks.

About 3½ dozen cookies

Sesame Seed Cookies

2 cups sifted all-purpose flour
½ teaspoon baking powder
½ cup sugar
⅔ cup lard
2 eggs
½ cup toasted or untoasted sesame
    seed*

1. Sift flour, baking powder, and sugar together into a bowl. Cut in lard with a pastry blender until particles are the size of rice kernels. Add 1 egg and mix until a dough is formed. Knead gently until smooth.
2. Form the dough into ½- to ¾-inch balls and flatten until about ¼ inch thick.
3. Separate remaining egg. Beat egg yolk and brush over top of each cookie; dip cookie, brushed side down, into the sesame seed and press the seed gently into the dough.
4. Brush lightly with remaining egg white, slightly beaten. Place on ungreased cookie sheets.
5. Bake at 325°F 12 to 15 minutes.

About 7½ dozen cookies

*To toast, put sesame seed into a pie pan and place in a 300°F oven for about 10 minutes, or until lightly browned; stir occasionally.

Walnut Bonnets

1 cup butter
¾ cup sugar
1 egg
1 teaspoon vanilla extract
2½ cups sifted all-purpose flour
½ teaspoon salt
¼ teaspoon baking powder
1 cup finely chopped walnuts
3 tablespoons apricot jam
    Glaze
    Candy sprinkles

1. Beat butter, sugar, egg, and vanilla extract together until light and fluffy.
2. Combine flour with salt and baking powder and blend into creamed mixture. Divide dough into thirds.
3. Mix walnuts and jam into one third of dough.
4. Using the remaining plain dough, fill pastry bag fitted with a No. 4 star tube and press out rings onto lightly greased baking sheets, making rings about 2¼ inches in diameter.
5. Fill centers of rings with the walnut dough, a rounded teaspoon for each.
6. Bake at 350°F about 15 minutes. Allow to cool.
7. If desired, brush centers with glaze and decorate with candy sprinkles.

About 3 dozen cookies

Glaze: Blend **1 cup sifted confectioners' sugar** with **1 tablespoon milk** and a drop or two of **vanilla extract.**

Thumbprint Cookies

1 cup butter
1½ teaspoons vanilla extract
½ cup sugar
1 egg yolk
1 tablespoon cream
2 cups sifted all-purpose flour
½ teaspoon baking powder
½ cup finely chopped pecans
1 egg white, slightly beaten
   Pecans, finely chopped (about ¾ cup)

1. Cream butter with extract; add sugar gradually, beating until fluffy. Beat in egg yolk with cream.
2. Sift flour and baking powder together; add to creamed mixture in fourths, mixing until blended after each addition. Stir in the ½ cup pecans.
3. Shape dough into 1-inch balls; dip into egg white and roll in remaining pecans.
4. Place 1 inch apart on ungreased cookie sheets, then press thumb into center of each.
5. Fill with **jelly, a red or green maraschino cherry half, or candied cherry half.**
6. Bake at 350°F 15 to 18 minutes.

About 4½ dozen cookies

Butter Crisps

1 cup butter
3 oz. cream cheese
1 teaspoon vanilla extract
1 cup sugar
1 egg yolk
2¼ cups sifted all-purpose flour
½ teaspoon salt
¼ teaspoon baking powder

1. Cream butter and cream cheese with extract; add sugar gradually, beating until fluffy. Add egg yolk and beat thoroughly.
2. Sift flour, salt, and baking powder together; add in fourths to creamed mixture, mixing until blended after each addition.
3. Following manufacturer's directions, fill a cookie press with dough and form cookies of varied shapes directly onto ungreased cookie sheets.
4. Bake at 350°F 12 to 15 minutes.
5. Cool on wire racks.

About 8 dozen cookies

Note: Dough may be tinted different colors, and before baking, the shapes may be sprinkled with colored sugar or with cinnamon-sugar. Cooled cookies may be decorated with tinted frosting.

Almond Spritz

1¼ cups butter
⅔ cup sugar
3 egg yolks (¼ cup)
¼ cup grated almonds
2½ cups sifted all-purpose flour

1. Cream butter; add sugar gradually, beating until fluffy. Add egg yolks, one at a time, beating thoroughly after each addition.
2. Stir in almonds. Add flour in fourths, mixing until blended after each addition.
3. Following manufacturer's directions, fill a cookie press with dough and form cookies of varied shapes directly onto ungreased cookie sheets.
4. Bake at 375°F 8 to 10 minutes.

About 6 dozen cookies

Filled Double Almond Spritz: Follow recipe for Almond Spritz, shaping cookies like ladyfingers. Lightly press **sliced almonds** onto tops. Bake; cool completely. Spread Rich Chocolate Filling, *page 30,* over bottoms of one half of the cookies; cover with remaining cookies.

Spritz

1 **cup butter**
1 **teaspoon vanilla extract**
½ **cup sugar**
1 **egg yolk**
2 **cups sifted all-purpose flour**
½ **teaspoon baking powder**
¼ **teaspoon salt**

1. Cream butter with extract; add sugar gradually, beating until fluffy. Add egg yolk and beat thoroughly.
2. Sift flour, baking powder, and salt together; add to creamed mixture in fourths, mixing until blended after each addition.
3. Following manufacturer's directions, fill a cookie press with dough and form cookies of varied shapes directly onto ungreased cookie sheets.
4. Bake at 350°F 12 minutes.

About 5 dozen cookies

Chocolate Spritz: Follow recipe for Spritz. Thoroughly blend ¼ **cup boiling water** and **6 tablespoons cocoa;** cool. Mix in after addition of egg yolk.

Nut Spritz: Follow recipe for Spritz. Stir in ½ **cup finely chopped nuts** (black walnuts or toasted blanched almonds) after the last addition of dry ingredients.

Chocolate-Tipped Spritz: Follow recipe for Spritz. Dip ends of cooled cookies into Chocolate Glaze I, *page 34.* If desired, dip into finely chopped **nuts,** crushed **peppermint stick candy,** or **chocolate shot.** Place on wire racks until glaze is set.

Marbled Spritz: Follow recipe for Spritz. Thoroughly blend **2 tablespoons boiling water** and **3 tablespoons cocoa;** cool. After the addition of egg yolk, remove a half of the creamed mixture to another bowl and mix in a half of the dry ingredients. Into remaining half of creamed mixture, stir cocoa mixture; blend in remaining dry ingredients. Shape each half of dough into a roll and cut lengthwise into halves. Press cut surfaces of vanilla and chocolate flavored doughs together before filling cookie press.

Spritz Sandwiches: Spread **chocolate frosting** or **jam** on bottom of some cookies. Cover with unfrosted cookies of same shape to form sandwiches.

Jelly-Filled Spritz: Make slight impression at center of cookie rounds and fill with ¼ **teaspoon jelly** or **jam** before baking.

Black Walnut Wafers

1 cup butter
1 teaspoon vanilla extract
2 cups firmly packed brown sugar
2 eggs
¾ cup black walnuts, finely chopped
2½ cups sifted all-purpose flour
1 teaspoon baking soda
1 teaspoon salt

1. Cream butter with extract; add brown sugar gradually, beating until fluffy. Add eggs, one at a time, beating thoroughly after each addition. Mix in black walnuts.
2. Sift flour, baking soda, and salt together. Add in fourths to creamed mixture, mixing until blended after each addition.
3. Shape dough into 1½-inch rolls. Wrap and chill several hours or overnight.
4. Remove one roll of dough at a time from refrigerator and cut into thin slices. Place slices 1½-inches apart on ungreased cookie sheets.
5. Bake at 350°F 8 minutes.

About 8 dozen cookies

Oasis Cookies

A cookie enhanced with dried figs, raisins, and citron.

1½ cups sifted all-purpose flour
½ teaspoon baking soda
½ teaspoon salt
½ teaspoon ground cinnamon
¼ teaspoon ground cloves
¼ teaspoon ground nutmeg
½ cup butter
½ teaspoon vanilla extract
1 cup firmly packed brown sugar
1 egg, well beaten
1½ teaspoons milk
¼ cup finely chopped dried figs
¼ cup finely chopped dark seedless raisins
2 tablespoons finely chopped candied citron

1. Sift flour, baking soda, salt, and spices together; set aside.
2. Cream butter with extract; add brown sugar gradually, beating until fluffy. Add a mixture of egg and milk and beat thoroughly.
3. Add dry ingredients in thirds, mixing until blended after each addition. Stir in fruits.
4. Chill dough until easy to handle.
5. Divide into halves; shape each portion into a 1½-inch roll. Wrap and chill several hours or overnight.
6. Cut into ⅛-inch slices; place 1½ inches apart on lightly greased cookie sheets.
7. Bake at 400°F 8 to 10 minutes.

About 8 dozen cookies

Fruity Sandwich Cookies: Follow recipe for Oasis Cookies. Omit chopped fruits, spices, and milk. Put through medium blade of food chopper **½ cup dried apricots, ½ cup pitted prunes,** and **¼ cup nuts;** blend in **1 tablespoon honey** (or enough to hold the mixture together). Shape into a 1¼-inch roll; wrap and chill thoroughly. Cut into thin slices, using a sharp knife (dip knife into flour to avoid sticking). Place a fruit slice between two slices of cookie dough; using a fork or fingers, press edges firmly together to seal.

My Favorite Cookie

This cookie, featuring pecans—native to the "Lone Star State"—is a favorite of Jean Houston Daniel, wife of a former governor of Texas. The recipe was given to Mrs. Daniel by her Great-Aunt Jennie, a granddaughter of General Sam Houston.

1 cup butter or margarine
1 cup sugar
1 cup firmly packed brown sugar
2 eggs, well beaten
1 teaspoon baking soda

1. Soften butter in a large bowl; add sugars gradually, beating until fluffy. Blend in eggs, baking soda, salt, and extract.
2. Stir in broken pecans and the flour until thoroughly mixed.
3. Tear off 6 pieces of waxed paper about 18 inches long. Divide the dough into 6 portions; put each portion onto a

1 teaspoon salt
1 teaspoon vanilla extract
2 cups broken pecans
4 cups sifted all-purpose flour

piece of waxed paper and shape into a 1½-inch roll. Wrap in waxed paper.
4. Chill until cold and firm.
5. Cut each roll into thin slices; place the waxed paper the dough was wrapped in on cookie sheets; transfer cookies to waxed paper-covered cookie sheets.
6. Bake at 350°F 5 to 7 minutes, or until light brown.
7. Remove cookies on waxed paper on which they were baked to a wire rack to cool. When cooled, remove cookies from paper.

3 to 4 dozen cookies per roll

Double Swirl Walnut Cookies

¾ cup shortening (half butter)
1¼ cups sugar
2 eggs
1 teaspoon vanilla extract
2½ cups sifted all-purpose flour
1 teaspoon baking powder
1 teaspoon salt
2 ounces (2 squares) unsweetened chocolate, melted
2 tablespoons milk
⅔ cup walnuts, finely chopped

1. Beat shortening, sugar, eggs, and vanilla extract together until fluffy.
2. Combine flour, baking powder, and salt; add to the creamed mixture and mix well.
3. Divide dough in half. To one half blend chocolate, milk, and ⅓ cup walnuts. To the remaining portion, mix in ⅓ cup walnuts. Wrap each half in waxed paper and chill thoroughly.
4. Roll the light dough on lightly floured surface to a 12×8-inch rectangle. Roll chocolate dough to same dimensions, and place light dough over chocolate dough, with shorter sides matching, longer side about ¼ inch from edge of chocolate. With a sharp knife, cut the dough in half crosswise, making two 6-inch sections for easier rolling.
5. Starting from the side with chocolate dough showing under the light dough, roll up the two together to the center. Turn over, and roll the dough from the other side to meet the first half. Wrap in waxed paper, plastic wrap, or foil, and place in freezer until dough is very firm.
6. Cut into ¼-inch slices and place on lightly greased cookie sheets.
7. Bake at 400°F 8 minutes. Leave cookies on cookie sheet for a minute, then remove carefully, using a broad spatula, and cool on wire racks.

About 4 dozen cookies

Note: If dough cracks on rolling, allow to stand at room temperature for a minute or two to warm up slightly. Cracks may be pinched together.

Coconut Classics

1 cup butter or margarine
½ teaspoon vanilla extract
1 cup sugar
1 egg
2 cups grated coconut
1¾ cups sifted all-purpose flour
½ teaspoon baking soda

1. Cream butter with extract; add sugar gradually, beating until fluffy. Add egg and beat well.
2. Thoroughly blend in 1¾ cups of the coconut.
3. Sift flour and baking soda together; add in fourths to creamed mixture, mixing well after each addition.
4. Chill dough until easy to handle.
5. Shape into six 1-inch rolls; coat with remaining coconut; wrap and chill at least 3 hours.
6. Cut each roll into ¼-inch slices; place ¾ inch apart on lightly greased cookie sheets.
7. Bake at 325°F about 15 minutes.

About 18 dozen cookies

Wheat Scotchies

1½ cups sifted all-purpose flour
1 teaspoon baking soda
½ teaspoon cream of tartar
½ teaspoon salt
½ cup finely crushed shredded wheat
¾ cup butter or margarine
½ teaspoon vanilla extract
1 cup firmly packed dark brown sugar
1 egg
½ cup raisins

1. Sift flour, baking soda, cream of tartar, and salt together; mix in crushed shredded wheat and set aside.
2. Cream butter with extract; add brown sugar gradually, beating until fluffy. Add egg and beat thoroughly.
3. Add the dry ingredients in fourths, mixing until well blended after each addition. Stir in the raisins.
4. Shape into 1½-inch rolls. Wrap each roll and chill several hours or overnight.
5. Cut each roll into ⅛-inch slices. Place about 1 inch apart on ungreased cookie sheets.
6. Bake at 375°F 6 to 8 minutes.

About 9 dozen cookies

Note: If desired, lightly brown the finely crushed shredded wheat in **1 tablespoon butter or margarine;** stir occasionally.

Rolled Cookies

If you want to cut a fancy figure, make rolled cookies. These are often baked for special occasions and during the holidays. Raisin-buttoned gingerbread men and decoratively iced Lebkuchen are rolled cookies. But so are Granny's sugar cookies and old-fashioned molasses cookies with their scalloped edge. They can be plain or partified—the trim will make the difference. ¶ Overhandling never helps a rolled cookie, so stir just until the

ingredients are mixed. Rolled cookies are made from a dough that is quite stiff; a soft, rich dough would be too sticky for this method.

Therein lies the problem many cooks have encountered when making rolled cookies. The dough tends to stick either to the rolling surface or to the rolling pan—or both. What to do?

Chilling the dough for a short time helps somewhat. A little flour on the rolling surface helps to prevent sticking, but too much flour in the dough makes a tough cookie, so don't overdo it. Just a little flour mixed with granulated sugar is better. Some cookie makers prefer sugar alone and others use confectioners' sugar. A pastry frame and stockinet cover for the rolling pin, both lightly rubbed with flour, simplify things.

Roll a little dough at a time, keeping the rest refrigerated while you work. Cut as many shapes from each rolling as you can, dipping the cutter into flour, then shaking off the excess, before each cut.

Don't reroll dough more than necessary. Save all the scraps, and roll them out together for one batch; bake the "in betweens" for family nibbling. Reworking tends to toughen the cookies.

The jigsaw puzzle cookie is a clever idea that

avoids any rerolling. Roll out a rectangle, then cut one large cookie shape that goes to all four sides; a Christmas tree or large doll shape, perhaps. Then cut odd shapes from the remnants for puzzle pieces. Bake the whole thing and decorate both the major shape and the smaller ones. Refit the puzzle on a heavy cardboard backing and cover with plastic wrap. Makes a whimsical gift or party favor.

Decorating, itself, can be the most fun of the whole baking project. Select a buttercream or confectioners' frosting that stays pliable while you are working, yet dries to a firmness that will hold further decorating, such as a fluted edge from a decorator bag, if you wish.

Make up a generous batch of frosting, and divide into several bowls, tinting each a different shade. When the cookies have cooled to room temperature, begin frosting. A table knife or butter knife with rounded edge works fine. Spread not quite to the edge, and not too thick, for quicker drying.

A thin glaze or heated fondant icing can be poured over cookies on a cake rack. Waxed paper underneath catches the overflow, which can be reused.

Chocolate-Almond Crescents

2½ cups sifted all-purpose flour
¼ cup sugar
½ teaspoon salt
1 cup butter, chilled and cut in pieces
1 cup blanched, toasted almonds, finely chopped
⅓ cup semisweet chocolate pieces, grated
2 egg yolks, slightly beaten
Confectioners' sugar

1. Blend flour, sugar, and salt in a bowl. Cut in the butter with pastry blender or two knives until particles are the size of rice kernels.
2. Mix in the almonds and chocolate. Add the egg yolks gradually, mixing thoroughly with a fork. Gather dough into a ball, working with fingertips until mixture holds together. Chill dough thoroughly.
3. Sift confectioners' sugar lightly and evenly over a flat surface. Roll a third of the dough about ¼ inch thick on the sugared surface. Cut with a lightly floured crescent-shaped cookie cutter. Transfer to lightly greased cookie sheets. Repeat for remaining dough.
4. Bake at 350°F about 7 minutes.
5. Immediately remove cookies to wire racks.

About 7 dozen cookies

Spicy Cinnamon Towers

Let the small fry assist in creating these "towers."

½ cup butter
¾ cup sugar
1 egg
1 tablespoon milk
2¼ cups sifted all-purpose flour
1½ teaspoons baking powder
1 teaspoon ground cinnamon
¼ teaspoon salt
¼ to ⅓ cup apple butter

1. Cream butter; add sugar gradually, beating until fluffy. Add egg and milk; beat well.
2. Sift flour, baking powder, cinnamon, and salt together. Add in fourths to creamed mixture, mixing until blended after each addition. Chill several hours, or until dough is firm enough to roll.
3. Remove amount of dough needed for single rolling and return remainder to refrigerator. Roll dough on a lightly floured surface to a thickness of not more than ¼ inch.
4. Using lightly floured scalloped cookie cutters that are 2 inches, 1¼ inches, and ¾ inch in diameter, cut out an equal number of cookies of the three sizes. Place cookies on ungreased cookie sheets. (Keeping cookies of one size together on sheets speeds the job of assembling cookie towers.)
5. Bake at 425°F 5 to 7 minutes.
6. Immediately and carefully remove cookies to wire racks to cool.
7. Using large cookies for bases of cookie towers, spoon ¼ to ½ teaspoon apple butter onto centers. Top with smaller-sized cookies. Spoon apple butter onto centers and top with smallest cookies.
8. Set cookie towers on waxed paper. Sift **confectioners' sugar** lightly over cookies.

About 2½ dozen cookie towers

Almond-Strawberry Towers: Follow recipe for Spicy Cinnamon Towers. Cut an equal number of cookies with 2-inch scalloped cookie cutter and with 1¼-inch round cookie cutter; omit ¾ inch cookies. Sprinkle smaller, unbaked cookies with crushed **rock candy.** Bake as directed. Substitute **strawberry jelly** for apple butter. Place a dot of jelly on center of each candy-sprinkled cookie; top with one **whole blanched almond.**

Melting Snowflakes

⅓ cup butter, chilled
1 cup sifted all-purpose flour
2 egg yolks
1 teaspoon cream
½ teaspoon almond extract
   Egg white, slightly beaten

1. Cut butter into flour until particles are the size of rice kernels.
2. Beat egg yolks, cream, and extract until very thick. Using a fork, blend into flour mixture in halves, mixing well after each addition. Chill dough thoroughly.
3. Roll dough ¼ inch thick on a floured surface; fold lengthwise in half, then crosswise in half; chill 1 hour.
4. Again roll dough ¼ inch thick. Cut with 1¼-inch round cutter. Transfer to ungreased cookie sheets. Brush rounds with egg white.
5. Bake at 350°F about 20 minutes.
6. Remove cookies to wire racks and sift with Vanilla Confectioners' Sugar, *below*.

About 2 dozen cookies

Vanilla Confectioners' Sugar: Cut a **vanilla bean** lengthwise, then crosswise, into pieces. Poke pieces into **1 to 2 pounds confectioners' sugar** at irregular intervals. Cover tightly and store. (The longer sugar stands, the richer the flavor.) When necessary, add more sugar. Replace vanilla bean when aroma is gone. Flavor **granulated sugar** this way, also.

Butter Sticks

¼ cup sugar
3 hard-cooked egg yolks, sieved
1 cup butter, softened
¼ teaspoon almond extract
2¼ cups sifted all-purpose flour

1. Add sugar gradually to sieved egg yolks, mixing well after each addition.
2. Add butter, a small amount at a time, beating until fluffy after each addition. Mix in extract.
3. Add flour in fourths, mixing until blended after each addition. Knead lightly with fingertips and form into a ball.
4. Roll a fourth of dough at a time ¼ inch thick on a floured surface.
5. Brush dough with slightly beaten **egg white;** sprinkle with a mixture of **ground cinnamon** and crushed **loaf sugar.** Cut into 4×¼-inch strips. Transfer to ungreased cookie sheets.
6. Bake at 350°F 8 to 10 minutes.

About 10 dozen cookies

Golden Sesame Cookies

½ cup butter
1 teaspoon vanilla extract
¾ cup confectioners' sugar
1 egg
1¼ cups sifted all-purpose flour
½ teaspoon baking powder
¼ teaspoon salt
¾ cup toasted sesame seeds*

1. Cream butter with extract; add confectioners' sugar gradually, beating until fluffy. Add egg and beat thoroughly.
2. Sift flour, baking powder, and salt; add in thirds to creamed mixture, mixing until blended after each addition; stir in sesame seed.
3. Chill dough thoroughly.
4. Roll a third of dough at a time ⅛ inch thick on a floured surface; cut with a 2-inch scalloped cutter. Transfer to ungreased cookie sheets.
5. Bake at 350°F 10 to 12 minutes.

About 4 dozen cookies

*To toast, put sesame seed into a pie pan and place in a 300°F oven for about 10 minutes, or until lightly browned; stir occasionally.

Milady's Fans

¾ cup butter
¼ teaspoon lemon extract
½ cup firmly packed brown sugar
2 egg yolks
2 cups sifted all-purpose flour
¼ teaspoon salt
1 tablespoon cream
2 oz. semisweet chocolate
¼ cup filberts, finely chopped

1. Cream butter with extract; add the brown sugar gradually, beating until fluffy. Add 1 egg yolk and beat thoroughly.
2. Blend flour and salt; add in fourths to creamed mixture, mixing until well blended after each addition.
3. Chill dough thoroughly.
4. Roll a third of dough at a time ⅛ inch thick on a lightly floured surface.
5. Cut with 3½-inch fluted cutter; cut each round into quarters; mark to resemble folds in a fan. Place fans on lightly greased cookie sheets and brush lightly with a mixture of 1 egg yolk and the cream.
6. Bake at 325°F 10 to 12 minutes.
7. Melt chocolate over hot water; cool.
8. When cookies are completely cooled, dip the pointed end of each into the cooled chocolate, then into chopped filberts.

About 4 dozen cookies

Autumn Leaves: Follow recipe for Milady's Fans. Shape dough into a 1½-inch roll. Cut slices ½ inch thick and mold each into a pear shape. Place on greased cookie sheets and flatten with palm of hand to ¼-inch thickness. Mark each to resemble veins in a leaf.

Double Daisies

1 cup butter
1½ teaspoons orange extract
1 cup confectioners' sugar
1 egg
2½ cups sifted all-purpose flour
1 teaspoon salt

Glaze and Frosting:
1 cup confectioners' sugar
2 tablespoons milk
½ teaspoon orange extract
Yellow food coloring
Cocoa

1. Cream butter with orange extract. Add confectioners' sugar gradually, creaming well. Add egg and beat thoroughly.
2. Mix flour and salt; add to creamed mixture and mix until well blended.
3. Chill dough thoroughly, 8 hours or overnight.
4. Using a small portion of chilled dough at a time, roll on a floured surface to ¼-inch thickness. Cut with floured large and small daisy cutters. Place on ungreased cookie sheets.
5. Bake at 375°F about 10 minutes, depending on size. Put on wire racks.
6. For glaze, combine confectioners' sugar, milk, and orange extract. Tint a pale yellow with food coloring.
7. Brush warm cookies with glaze. Cool.
8. Mix a small amount of cocoa and additional confectioners' sugar with remaining glaze to make the consistency of frosting.
9. Put a small amount of frosting on center of each large cookie. Top with a small one. Decorate top with a small amount of frosting.

About 2½ dozen cookies

Texas Cookies

A recipe from Mrs. Lyndon B. Johnson, former First Lady of the United States.

½ cup butter
1 tablespoon grated lemon peel
½ teaspoon lemon extract

1. Cream butter with lemon peel and extract; add sugar gradually, beating until fluffy. Add egg and beat thoroughly. Mix in cream.

1 cup sugar
1 egg
1 tablespoon cream
1½ cups sifted all-purpose flour
1 teaspoon baking powder
½ teaspoon salt

2. Sift remaining ingredients together; add in thirds to creamed mixture, mixing until blended after each addition.
3. Chill dough 2 to 3 hours, or overnight.
4. Roll a small portion of dough at a time very thin on a lightly floured surface. Cut with a state-of-Texas-shaped cutter or other large cookie cutter. Transfer to ungreased cookie sheets.
5. Bake at 375°F 8 to 10 minutes.
6. Cool cookies on wire racks.

About 5 dozen cookies

Butter Pecan Shortbread

Shortbread:
1 cup butter
½ cup firmly packed light brown sugar
2¼ cups all-purpose flour
½ cup finely chopped pecans

Decorator Icing:
2 tablespoons butter
¼ teaspoon vanilla extract
1 cup confectioners' sugar
Milk (about 1 tablespoon)
Red and green food coloring

1. To prepare shortbread, beat butter until softened; add brown sugar gradually, beating until fluffy. Add flour gradually, beating until well blended. Mix in pecans.
2. Chill dough until easy to handle.
3. On a lightly floured surface, pat and roll dough into a 14×10-inch rectangle about ¼ inch thick. Cut dough into 24 squares. Divide each square into 4 triangles.
4. Transfer triangles to ungreased cookie sheets.
5. Bake at 300°F 18 to 20 minutes, or until lightly browned. Remove to wire racks to cool.
6. To prepare icing, cream butter with vanilla extract in a small bowl. Add confectioners' sugar gradually, beating until blended. Blend in enough milk for desired consistency for icing. Color one third of icing red and two thirds green. Force icing through a decorator tube to make a holly decoration on each cookie.

8 dozen cookies

Almond Crisscrosses

2 cups sifted all-purpose flour
1 teaspoon baking powder
¾ cup sugar
1 cup butter, chilled and cut in pieces
1 egg yolk, slightly beaten
Almond Filling, *below*

1. Sift flour, baking powder, and sugar together into a bowl. Cut in the butter until mixture becomes a soft dough (requires working beyond the stage when particles are the size of rice kernels). Blend in the egg yolk.
2. Shape dough into a ball, kneading lightly with fingertips until mixture holds together.
3. Spread two thirds of the dough evenly over bottom and up ¼ inch on the sides of a 13×9×2-inch baking pan. Spread Almond Filling over dough; set aside.
4. Roll remaining dough ⅛ inch thick on a floured surface. Using a pastry wheel, cut into strips ¾ inch wide. Arrange strips to make a lattice design over the filling.
5. Bake at 350°F 35 to 40 minutes.
6. While still warm, cut into bars.

About 4 dozen cookies

Almond Filling: Blend **1 cup confectioners' sugar,** ½ **teaspoon ground cardamom,** and ½ **teaspoon ground cinnamon.** Stir in ¾ **cup unblanched almonds,** grated. Add a mixture of **1 egg white** and **2 tablespoons water;** mix thoroughly.

Cream Cheese Dainties

Apricot, Strawberry, or
    Mincemeat Filling, *below*
½ cup butter
1 package (3 ounces) cream cheese
1 teaspoon sugar
1 cup all-purpose flour

1. Prepare desired filling or fillings and set aside.
2. Beat butter and cream cheese until well blended. Mix in sugar and then flour. Divide dough in half and chill thoroughly.
3. On a lightly floured surface, roll each half of dough to $1/16$-inch thickness. Use floured 2-inch cookie cutters to cut about 3 dozen "bases."
4. Transfer bases to cookie sheets. Spoon about ¼ teaspoon filling in center of each cookie.
5. Cut remaining dough with the same size cutters. Use 1-inch cutters to cut out the centers. Top cookie bases with cut-out cookies or with 1-inch cutouts.
6. Bake at 375°F 6 to 8 minutes. Remove immediately to wire racks to cool.

About 5 dozen cookies

Apricot Filling: Mix ½ cup apricot preserves with ½ teaspoon lemon extract.

Strawberry Filling: Mix ½ cup strawberry preserves with ½ teaspoon almond extract.

Mincemeat Filling: Mix ½ cup prepared mincemeat with ½ teaspoon orange extract.

Note: If desired, make tart shells from dough. Roll dough to $1/16$-inch thickness and cut out rounds with a 2¾-inch cookie cutter. Carefully line well-buttered 2¼×¾-inch tart pan wells with rounds of dough; prick with a fork. Bake at 375°F 8 to 10 minutes, or until lightly browned. Cool; remove from pans. Fill with fruit or cream filling.

About 3 dozen tart shells

Vienna Wafers

2 cups sifted all-purpose flour
⅔ cup sugar
    Few grains salt
½ cup plus 2 tablespoons butter
½ cup blanched almonds, ground
1 teaspoon vanilla extract
1 egg, well beaten
1 tablespoon egg white
½ cup confectioners' sugar
½ cup apricot preserves, heated

1. Blend flour, sugar, and salt; cut in the butter until particles are the size of rice kernels.
2. Stir in almonds and extract. Mix in egg; knead with fingertips until a soft dough is formed. Cover and set aside 1 hour.
3. Divide dough into halves; place each half in center of an ungreased cookie sheet and roll ⅛ inch thick into a square, about 7×7 inches. Set aside.
4. For icing, beat egg white until frothy; add confectioners' sugar gradually, beating constantly until mixture stands in peaks.
5. Using pastry bag and No. 2 decorating tube, pipe icing onto one square to form a lattice design.
6. Bake both squares at 350°F 15 minutes.
7. Remove undecorated cookie square to wire rack; spread warm preserves evenly over surface. Carefully place decorated square on top. Cool; sprinkle with confectioners' sugar. Cut into squares.

About 2½ dozen cookies

Old-Fashioned Spice Cookies

2 cups sifted all-purpose flour
¾ teaspoon salt
½ teaspoon baking soda
1 teaspoon cinnamon
½ teaspoon nutmeg
¼ teaspoon cloves
1 cup soft vegetable shortening
1 cup firmly packed brown sugar
½ cup granulated sugar
1 egg
2 tablespoons water
2 cups uncooked rolled oats, quick or old-fashioned
¾ cup currants

1. Blend flour, salt, baking soda, and spices in a bowl. Add shortening, sugars, egg, and water; beat with electric mixer until smooth (about 2 minutes). Stir in oats and currants.
2. Chill dough thoroughly.
3. Roll only a small portion of chilled dough at a time to ⅛-inch thickness on a pastry canvas or board lightly sprinkled with **confectioners' sugar.** Cut with a floured 3-inch round cutter. Put onto ungreased cookie sheets. Sprinkle with **granulated sugar.**
4. Bake at 375°F 8 to 10 minutes.

About 5 dozen cookies

Almond Meringue-Topped Cookies

½ cup unsalted butter
3 tablespoons sugar
3 egg yolks, beaten
¾ cup sifted all-purpose flour
2 egg whites
⅛ teaspoon salt
½ cup sugar
¾ teaspoon vanilla extract
¾ teaspoon grated lemon peel
⅓ cup blanched, shredded almonds

1. Cream butter; add 3 tablespoons sugar gradually, beating until fluffy. Add egg yolks and beat thoroughly.
2. Add flour in halves, mixing until blended after each addition.
3. Roll dough about ¼ inch thick on well-floured surface; cut with 1½-inch round cutter. Transfer rounds to ungreased cookie sheets; set aside.
4. Beat egg whites and salt until frothy; add ½ cup sugar gradually, beating constantly until stiff peaks are formed. Fold in the extract, lemon peel, and almonds.
5. Top each cookie round with a heaping teaspoonful of meringue, shaping into a peak.
6. Bake at 325°F 20 minutes.

About 2½ dozen cookies

Coffee-Chocolate Ringles

2 oz. (2 sq.) unsweetened chocolate
1¾ cups sifted all-purpose flour
2 teaspoons baking powder
⅛ teaspoon salt
1 tablespoon instant coffee
¼ teaspoon ground cinnamon
⅔ cup butter
½ teaspoon vanilla extract
1 cup sugar
1 egg

1. Melt chocolate; set aside to cool.
2. Sift flour, baking powder, salt, instant coffee, and cinnamon together; set aside.
3. Cream butter with extract; add sugar gradually, beating until fluffy. Add egg and beat thoroughly. Blend in cooled chocolate.
4. Add dry ingredients in fourths, mixing until blended after each addition. Chill thoroughly.
5. Roll one third of dough at a time ¼ inch thick on a floured surface or between two sheets of waxed paper; cut with 1½-inch scalloped cutter. Cut out centers, if desired.
6. Transfer to ungreased cookie sheets and sprinkle tops with **sugar.**
7. Bake at 350°F about 10 minutes.

About 6½ dozen cookies

Frosted Almond Leaf Cookies

¾ cup (6 oz.) almond paste
3 tablespoons cold water
⅛ teaspoon almond extract
1 egg white, unbeaten
1¼ cups sifted all-purpose flour
1 cup confectioners' sugar
¼ teaspoon salt
  Chocolate Glaze II, *page 22* (use ¼ recipe)

1. Force almond paste, a little at a time, through a sieve into a bowl. Gradually work a mixture of water and extract into almond paste, using back of wooden spoon. Mix in egg white.
2. Combine the flour, confectioners' sugar, and salt. Add in fourths to almond-paste mixture, mixing until blended after each addition.
3. Turn dough onto a pastry canvas sprinkled with **confectioners' sugar.** Roll about ⅛ inch thick. Cut with leaf-shaped cookie cutter or pattern prepared from a piece of cardboard. (Leaf should be 4½×2½ inches) If using cardboard pattern, lay it over dough and with a sharp knife carefully cut around it. Transfer to generously greased cookie sheets.
4. Bake at 350°F 5 to 6 minutes, or until delicately browned.
5. Using spatula, immediately remove to wire racks. Spread glaze thinly over cooled cookies. Let glaze set partially and with point of a knife mark veins in leaves; if necessary, place in refrigerator just long enough for chocolate to set.

About 2½ dozen cookies

Walnut Cakes

1¼ cups sifted all-purpose flour
⅓ cup sugar
½ cup butter
2 tablespoons milk
½ teaspoon vanilla extract
½ cup chopped walnuts
1 to 1½ cups walnut halves and large pieces
  Glaze, *below*
4 ounces (4 squares) semisweet chocolate

1. Combine flour and sugar. Cut butter into mixture until particles are very fine.
2. Sprinkle milk and vanilla extract over mixture, and mix to a stiff dough. Mix in chopped walnuts.
3. Roll dough ¼ inch thick on a lightly floured surface, and cut into rounds. Place on ungreased cookie sheet.
4. Cover each cookie with walnut halves or large pieces, pressing the nuts lightly into the dough.
5. Bake at 350°F 15 minutes. Remove cookies to wire rack and place rack on a cookie sheet. Spoon tops with hot glaze, and allow cookies to cool.
6. Melt chocolate over warm, not hot, water and spread each cookie bottom with chocolate. Place cookies on waxed paper until chocolate is set.

1 dozen 3-inch cookies,
2 dozen 2-inch cookies, or
3½ dozen 1½-inch cookies

Glaze: Combine ⅓ **cup firmly packed dark brown sugar** and ⅓ **cup light corn syrup** in a small saucepan. Bring to boiling and use immediately.

Grandmother's Jelly Cookies

1⅓ cups sifted all-purpose flour
½ teaspoon salt
½ cup butter
½ teaspoon vanilla extract
⅓ cup sugar
1 egg yolk
1 egg white, slightly beaten

1. Blend flour and salt; set aside.
2. Cream butter with extract; add ⅓ cup sugar gradually, beating until fluffy. Add egg yolk; beat thoroughly.
3. Add dry ingredients in halves, mixing until blended after each addition.
4. Chill dough for easier handling, if desired.
5. Roll one half of dough at a time ⅛ inch thick on a floured

Pepparkakor, 74;
Butter Pecan Shortbread, 61;
Cream Cheese Dainties, 62

¼ **cup blanched almonds, finely chopped**
¼ **cup sugar**
⅓ **cup jelly**

surface; cut 16 rounds with a 2½-inch cutter from half of dough; place on ungreased cookie sheet.
6. Bake at 375°F 10 to 12 minutes.
7. Meanwhile, cut 16 shapes from remaining dough, using fancy-shaped cutter slightly less than 2½ inches; cut a ½-inch round from center of each. (Bake ½-inch rounds for samplers.)
8. Brush tops with egg white; sprinkle with a mixture of the almonds and ¼ cup sugar.
9. Bake at 375°F about 10 minutes.
10. Cool; spoon 1 teaspoon jelly onto center of each round cookie and top with fancy-shaped cookie.

16 double cookies

Celestial Cookies

A heavenly walnut-filled sour cream cookie made from a very rich yeast dough.

1 **pkg. active dry yeast**
¼ **cup warm water**
4 **cups sifted all-purpose flour**
2 **tablespoons sugar**
½ **teaspoon salt**
1 **cup butter, chilled**
2 **egg yolks**
⅛ **teaspoon vanilla extract**
1 **cup dairy sour cream**
Nut Filling, *below*

1. Soften yeast in the warm water; set aside.
2. Blend flour, sugar, and salt in a bowl. Cut in butter with a pastry blender or two knives until particles are the size of rice kernels; set aside.
3. Beat egg yolks and extract until thick. Add yeast and sour cream gradually, beating well after each addition.
4. Add to the flour-butter mixture gradually, blending well after each addition. Cover and chill overnight.
5. The next day prepare Nut Filling; set aside.
6. Roll a half of dough at a time into a 16×12-inch rectangle on a floured surface. Spread surface of dough with filling.
7. Roll the other half of dough to the same size on waxed paper. Invert dough on waxed paper over filling; press down gently and evenly; peel off paper.
8. Cut into 2-inch squares or into bars or triangles; press edges together to seal. Place on lightly greased cookie sheets.
9. Bake at 350°F 15 minutes.

About 4 dozen cookies

Nut Filling: Blend **1½ cups walnuts**, grated, with **1 cup plus 2 tablespoons sugar.** Gradually add **3 egg whites,** slightly beaten, and ¼ **teaspoon vanilla extract,** blending well after each addition.

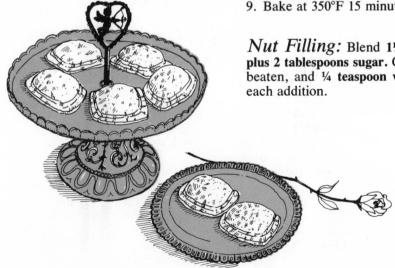

Sand Tarts

This particular recipe is a Pennsylvania Dutch favorite. However, variations of the butter-rich cookie appear in several European countries, and in England and Scotland, where it is known as shortbread.

2 cups butter
2½ cups sugar
2 eggs
4 cups sifted all-purpose flour
1 egg white, slightly beaten

1. Cream butter; add sugar gradually, beating until fluffy. Add eggs one at a time, beating thoroughly after each addition.
2. Add flour in fourths, mixing until well blended after each addition. Chill dough overnight.
3. Removing from refrigerator only amount needed for a single rolling, roll dough about ¹/₁₆ inch thick on a floured surface; cut with 2-inch round or fancy cutter. Brush tops with egg white; sprinkle with a mixture of ½ **cup sugar** and **2 teaspoons ground cinnamon.**
4. Transfer to ungreased cookie sheets; press a quarter of **pecan** onto center of each cookie.
5. Bake at 350°F about 9 minutes.

About 17½ dozen cookies

Brown Moravian Cookies

A Pennsylvania Dutch cookie.

4 cups sifted all-purpose flour
¼ teaspoon baking soda
¼ teaspoon salt
1 teaspoon ground cinnamon
½ teaspoon ground cloves
¼ teaspoon ground ginger
1 cup firmly packed light brown sugar
½ cup butter
½ cup lard*
1½ cups light molasses
½ teaspoon cider vinegar

1. Sift flour, baking soda, salt, and spices together into a large bowl. Add brown sugar; mix well.
2. Cut in butter and lard. Add molasses and vinegar gradually, mixing well. Chill dough thoroughly.
3. Using a small amount of dough at a time, roll out about ⅛-inch thick on a lightly floured surface. Cut with fancy cookie cutters. Transfer to greased cookie sheets.
4. Bake at 350°F 8 to 10 minutes.

About 6 dozen cookies
*Use butter, if desired, but then cookie will not be authentic.

Filled Crescents

1 cup sifted all-purpose flour
¼ teaspoon salt
½ cup butter, chilled
1 hard-cooked egg yolk, sieved
⅓ cup sugar
1 tablespoon dairy sour cream
1 teaspoon vanilla extract
¼ cup apricot preserves

1. Blend flour and salt in a bowl. Cut in butter until mixture becomes a soft dough (requires working beyond the stage when particles are the size of rice kernels).
2. Blend in sieved egg yolk, sugar, sour cream, and extract. Knead lightly with fingertips and form into a ball.
3. Roll a half of the dough at a time into a 10-inch round on a floured surface; cut into 12 wedge-shaped pieces.
4. Spread ½ teaspoon preserves on wide part of each wedge; roll up, starting at outer edge. Place on ungreased cookie sheet with point underneath; curve into a crescent.
5. Bake at 375°F 10 to 12 minutes.
6. Remove to wire racks to cool slightly. While still warm, sift Vanilla Confectioners' Sugar, *page 59,* over cookies.

2 dozen cookies

Holiday Cookies

Those restless nights between Thanksgiving and Christmas could be the work of the Ghost of Christmas Past, conjuring up visions of cookies "like Mother used to make." Not even a Scrooge would deny the children of Christmas Present the thrill of those same traditional treats. Let them share in the baking, too, and they'll have memories to savor through many Christmases-Yet-To-Come. ¶ Some of the recipes gathered here would be just as much at home in our "Around the World" collection, because of the heirloom nature of holiday cookies. Their origins go back in time and across continents. But these particular recipes have special holiday associations, and will probably take priority in Christmas baking.

One portion of the holiday baking goes for gifts to the teacher, scout mother, and neighbor. Other cookies will be set aside for guests, and others for family meals. The ones that don't quite measure up (a little too brown, or a broken corner) will be eaten on the spot. No one ever minds these mistakes. (More than a few are intentional.)

Some cookies are baked "for show." These are hung from branches of the tree, or as a mobile. You can decorate these long and lavishly, knowing that they will endure—at least, a little longer than most.

Those baked for gifts can be presented in containers that reflect your creativity, too. Plan ahead and save cans with reusable lids—coffee and shortening cans are ideal. When empty, wash and save them for some afternoon when you have time to decorate them. Then cover them with colorful adhesive-backed paper for a canister that will last.

Cookies not only provide refreshments for holiday entertaining; they can provide a party theme. In some neighborhoods, a cookie exchange has become a custom. Each guest is asked to bake up a large batch of her favorite cookie in advance of the party, and to divide it into small packets for each of the other guests to take home. Sometimes copies of the recipe are requested for each packet. This saves the neighbors the many hours of baking time it would take to produce such a bright assortment. And each recipe file is enriched with the most favored recipes of several friends.

Much as we associate holiday cookies with Christmas, there are other holidays all through the year. They can be observed with cookies dedicated to the spirit of the occasion, such as egg-shaped cookies for Easter and Pumpkin Jumbos for Halloween. Each holiday will mean more when you take time out to honor it with cookies you have made yourself.

Or, buy inexpensive gift items that can double as cookie containers. A small basket, or basket plate such as those used to support paper plates, is nice. Apothecary jars show off the cookies to good advantage, too. So do brandy snifters, clear plastic flowerpots, and mugs.

Love Letters (Szerelmes Levél)

Rich pastry squares folded like envelopes, with a nut-meringue filling inside, become Hungarian "love letters," a Valentine's Day treat.

2 cups sifted all-purpose flour
2 tablespoons sugar
¼ teaspoon salt
¾ cup butter, chilled
4 egg yolks, slightly beaten
½ cup coarsely chopped walnuts
1 teaspoon grated lemon peel
2 egg whites
¼ cup sugar
½ teaspoon ground cinnamon

1. Blend flour, sugar, and salt. Cut in butter until particles are the size of rice kernels.
2. Add egg yolks gradually, blending with a fork (mixture will be crumbly). Knead lightly with fingertips and shape into a ball.
3. Divide dough into halves; wrap in waxed paper and chill 1 hour.
4. Mix walnuts and lemon peel; set aside.
5. Fifteen minutes before chilling time is ended, beat egg whites until frothy. Add a mixture of sugar and cinnamon gradually, beating well after each addition; beat until stiff peaks are formed.
6. Gently fold in nut mixture; set aside.
7. Roll one half of dough at a time ⅛ inch thick on a floured surface; cut into 3-inch squares.
8. Put about 2 teaspoons of filling onto center of each square; bring opposite corners together, overlapping slightly at center; repeat with other two corners.
9. Transfer to ungreased cookie sheets. Brush tops with slightly beaten **egg.**
10. Bake at 350°F about 20 minutes.
11. Cool cookies on wire racks. Sift a mixture of **2 to 3 tablespoons confectioners' sugar** and **½ to 1 teaspoon ground cinnamon** over cooled cookies.

About 2½ dozen cookies

Norwegian Cones (Krumkaker)

This traditional Christmas confection is extremely fragile, so handle and store it carefully.

1½ cups sifted all-purpose flour
½ cup cornstarch
1½ teaspoons ground cardamom
1 cup butter
1¼ cups sugar
3 egg yolks
3 egg whites
⅛ teaspoon salt

1. Blend flour, cornstarch, and cardamom.
2. Cream butter; add sugar gradually, beating until fluffy. Add egg yolks, one at a time, beating thoroughly after each addition.
3. Add dry ingredients in fourths, mixing until blended after each addition.
4. Beat egg whites and salt until stiff peaks are formed; gently fold into batter.
5. Heat krumkake iron (usually available in the housewares section of department stores) following manufacturer's instructions, until a drop of water "sputters" on hot surface.
6. For each, spoon 1½ to 2 teaspoons batter onto hot iron; close the iron and bake on each side for a few minutes, or until lightly browned.
7. Using a spatula, immediately remove wafer and roll into cone. Cool completely.

About 4 dozen cookies

Belgian Christmas Cookies

⅔ cup butter
1 teaspoon almond extract
1 cup firmly packed dark brown
  sugar
2 eggs
1⅔ cups sifted all-purpose flour
1½ teaspoons baking powder
½ teaspoon salt
½ cup finely chopped unblanched
  almonds
½ teaspoon ground cinnamon
2 teaspoons red sugar
2 teaspoons green sugar

1. Cream butter with extract; add brown sugar gradually, creaming until fluffy. Add eggs, one at a time, beating thoroughly after each addition.
2. Sift flour, baking powder, and salt together; add in thirds to creamed mixture, mixing until blended after each addition. Turn into a greased 15×10×1-inch jelly roll pan and spread evenly to edges.
3. Sprinkle a mixture of almonds and cinnamon over batter, then sprinkle with a mixture of red and green sugars.
4. Bake at 375°F 10 to 12 minutes.
5. Cut into bars while still warm.

About 5 dozen cookies

Passover Cookies

¼ cup shortening
1 teaspoon grated lemon peel
1 cup sugar
6 eggs
1 cup matzo cake meal
⅔ cup ground toasted filberts
2 tablespoons potato starch
⅛ teaspoon salt

1. Cream shortening with lemon peel. Add sugar gradually, beating constantly. Add eggs, one at a time, beating until light and fluffy after each addition.
2. Combine cake meal, ground filberts, potato starch, and salt; fold into creamed mixture, a little at a time.
3. Drop by tablespoonfuls onto ungreased cookie sheets. Sprinkle lightly with **sugar** and press a whole **filbert** into center of each cookie.
4. Bake at 400°F about 10 minutes, or until lightly browned.
5. Remove from cookie sheets immediately and cool on wire racks.

About 3½ dozen cookies

Jan Hagel

These Dutch delicacies are popular throughout the holiday season and particularly on the feast day of Saint Nicholas.

1 cup butter
1 cup sugar
1 egg yolk
2 cups sifted all-purpose flour
¼ teaspoon salt
1 egg white
4 pieces loaf sugar, finely crushed
½ teaspoon ground cinnamon
½ cup finely chopped nuts

1. Cream butter; add sugar gradually, beating until fluffy. Add egg yolk and beat well.
2. Blend flour and salt; add in fourths to creamed mixture, mixing until blended after each addition.
3. Divide dough into halves and roll each on an ungreased cookie sheet into a 12×10-inch rectangle.
4. Beat egg white slightly with a small amount of **water**; brush lightly over dough. Mix crushed sugar with cinnamon and nuts; sprinkle over each rectangle.
5. Bake at 375°F 15 minutes.
6. Trim the edges and cut into bars while warm.

About 4 dozen cookies

Carnival Pancakes *(Fastnacht Kuchlein)*

The Swiss Mardi Gras, called Fasching, is celebrated for two weeks prior to the Lenten season. These traditional "little cakes" highlight the festivities. These inviting deep-fried "cakes" beckon from every pastry shop window to all passersby.

2 tablespoons butter, melted
¼ cup milk
¼ cup heavy cream
½ teaspoon salt
1 teaspoon kirsch
4 eggs
3⅓ cups sifted all-purpose flour
¼ cup cornstarch
    Lard for deep frying

1. Combine butter, milk, cream, salt, kirsch, and eggs in a bowl and beat thoroughly.
2. Blend flour and cornstarch; add about ½ cup at a time to egg mixture, mixing until well blended after each addition. Chill dough thoroughly.
3. Heat lard to 365° to 370°F.
4. Divide dough into 32 equal portions and cover until ready to use. Roll each into a "two-hand" size round.
5. Sprinkle one round liberally with **flour,** then place another on top and roll ¹/₁₆ inch thick. Separate carefully; brush off excess flour and place each round between pieces of waxed paper. Repeat with all portions of dough before starting to deep fry.
6. Deep fry each round in hot fat 1 to 2 minutes, or until golden brown, turning once. Drain over fat a few seconds, then remove to absorbent paper; cool.
7. Sprinkle with **confectioners' sugar.**

32 (8-inch) pancakes

Note: If desired, roll out dough the day before, place between sheets of waxed paper, and refrigerate overnight. Deep fry the next day as needed.

Peppernuts *(Pfeffernüsse)*

In this recipe that famous spicy German favorite has been given a slightly different twist . . . the flavor of brandy permeates both cookie and frosting.

2 cups all-purpose flour
⅛ teaspoon salt
⅛ teaspoon black pepper
1 teaspoon ground cinnamon
¼ teaspoon ground allspice
¼ teaspoon ground cloves
¼ teaspoon ground nutmeg
⅛ teaspoon ground mace
¼ cup blanched almonds, grated
2 eggs
1 cup sugar
¼ cup chopped candied citron
    Brandy
    Frosting, *below*

1. Sift flour, salt, and spices together and blend in the almonds; set aside.
2. Beat eggs and sugar until very thick.
3. Add dry ingredients in thirds, mixing until well blended after each addition. Stir in the citron.
4. Roll dough ½ inch thick on a floured surface; cut with 1-inch round cutter. Place on lightly greased cookie sheet; put a drop of brandy on the center of each cutout.
5. Bake at 350°F 12 to 15 minutes.
6. Frost cookies while still warm. Cool on racks before storing. To soften cookies, store for several days with a piece of apple or orange.

About 5½ dozen cookies

Frosting: Mix **1 cup confectioners' sugar, 1 teaspoon brandy,** and **4 to 5 teaspoons water** until smooth.

About ⅓ cup

Currant Cakes

A Pennsylvania Dutch Christmas cookie.

2 cups butter
2 teaspoons grated lemon peel
2 tablespoons lemon juice
2¼ cups sugar
6 eggs, well beaten
3¼ cups sifted all-purpose flour
¼ teaspoon salt
½ lb. (1½ cups) currants

1. Cream butter with lemon peel and juice; add sugar gradually, beating until fluffy. Add eggs in thirds, beating thoroughly after each addition.
2. Blend flour and salt; add to creamed mixture in thirds, mixing until blended after each addition. Mix in the currants.
3. Drop by teaspoonfuls onto large well-greased cookie sheets, spreading batter for each cookie very thinly.
4. Bake at 350°F 10 minutes.

About 7½ dozen cookies

Danish Christmas Crullers I (Klejner)

5 egg yolks
1 egg
1 cup sugar
5 teaspoons finely shredded lemon peel
3¾ cups sifted all-purpose flour
½ cup heavy cream
Lard for deep frying

1. Combine egg yolks, egg, sugar, and lemon peel. Beat until very thick. Beating only until smooth after each addition, alternately add flour in thirds and cream in halves. Chill thoroughly.
2. About 20 minutes before ready to deep fry, start heating lard to 365°F.
3. Working with a small amount of dough at a time (keep remainder of dough chilled) on a floured surface, knead dough until smooth and roll it out thin. Cut into 3×1½-inch strips, slanting the ends. Cut a slit about 1½ inches long in center of each strip and draw one end through the slit.
4. Fry in the hot fat until golden brown, turning once.
5. Remove to absorbent paper and drain thoroughly before serving or storing.

8 to 12 dozen cookies
(depending on thickness)

Danish Christmas Crullers II: Follow recipe for Danish Christmas Crullers I. Omit lemon peel and blend ½ to 1 teaspoon ground cardamom with the flour.

Holly Cheese Cakes

Filling:
3 packages (8 ounces each) cream cheese
1½ teaspoons vanilla extract
1 cup sugar
5 eggs

Topping:
1 pint dairy sour cream
¼ cup sugar
1 teaspoon vanilla extract

Decoration:
Red and green candied cherries, cut in pieces

1. Line 1½-inch muffin pan wells with fluted paper cups.
2. For filling, cream the cheese with vanilla extract. Add sugar and eggs; beat well. Spoon about 1 tablespoon mixture into each paper cup.
3. Bake at 350°F about 20 minutes, or until top cracks slightly.
4. Meanwhile, for topping, combine sour cream, sugar, and vanilla extract.
5. Spoon a small amount of topping onto each cake. Bake 5 minutes. Cool on racks.
6. Decorate with red and green cherry pieces to resemble holly. Refrigerate until ready to serve.

6½ to 7 dozen cakes

Fattigmann

A traditional Norwegian Christmas favorite.

10 **egg yolks**
2 **egg whites**
¾ **cup sugar**
¼ **cup brandy**
1 **cup heavy cream**
5 **cups sifted all-purpose flour**
2 **teaspoons ground cardamom**
   Lard for deep frying

1. Beat egg yolks, egg whites, sugar, and brandy until very thick. Add cream slowly, stirring well.
2. Sift flour and cardamom together; add about ½ cup at a time to egg mixture, mixing thoroughly after each addition. Wrap and chill overnight.
3. Heat lard to 365° to 370°F in a deep saucepan.
4. Roll dough, a small portion at a time, ¹/₁₆ inch thick on a floured surface.
5. Using a floured knife or pastry wheel, cut into diamond shapes, 5×2 inches; make a lengthwise slit in the center of each diamond. Pull the tip of one end through each slit and tuck back under itself.
6. Deep fry 1 to 2 minutes, or until golden brown, turning once. Drain and cool.
7. Sprinkle cookies with **confectioners' sugar.** Store in tightly covered containers.

About 6 dozen cookies

Cinnamon Stars (Zimtsterne)

The rich blend of almond and cinnamon flavor adds a touch of distinction to this star-shaped confection, a German-Swiss holiday favorite.

⅓ **cup plus 1 tablespoon egg whites**
1 **cup confectioners' sugar**
1 **teaspoon grated lemon peel**
¾ **teaspoon ground cinnamon**
2 **cups unblanched almonds, grated**

1. Lightly grease 2 cookie sheets, sprinkle with **flour,** and shake off excess; set aside.
2. Using an electric beater, beat egg whites until stiff, not dry, peaks are formed. Add confectioners' sugar gradually, beating 5 minutes at medium speed. Remove ⅓ cup of meringue and set aside.
3. Into remaining meringue, beat the lemon peel and cinnamon. Fold in the almonds.
4. Turn almond mixture onto a pastry canvas sprinkled with **confectioners'** or **granulated sugar.** Gently roll ¼ to ⅜ inch thick. Lightly sprinkle with sugar. Cut with a 2-inch star-shaped cookie cutter dipped in confectioners' sugar.
5. Transfer to cookie sheets; drop about ½ teaspoonful of reserved meringue onto each star and spread out evenly onto points. Set aside in a warm place (about 80°F) 1½ hours.
6. Bake at 375°F 5 minutes.

About 3 dozen cookies

Basler Brunsli

As appropriate to Christmas as it is uniquely Swiss (Basler translates "from Basle"), this rich cookie will be one of your great joys of the season.

1 lb. unblanched almonds, grated*
(5 cups)
4 to 4½ oz. (4 to 4½ sq.)
unsweetened chocolate, grated*
2½ cups sugar
1 teaspoon ground cinnamon
1 tablespoon kirsch
4 egg whites (about ⅔ cup)

1. Thoroughly blend almonds and chocolate with a mixture of sugar and cinnamon. Drizzle with the kirsch.
2. Beat the egg whites until stiff, not dry, peaks are formed. Blend into nut mixture. Chill thoroughly.
3. Roll a fourth of the mixture at a time ½ inch thick on a lightly sugared surface. Cut with 1¼-inch round cutter. Place on lightly greased cookie sheets.
4. Bake at 300°F 15 minutes. Cool on wire racks.

About 10 dozen cookies

*Blender grating speeds the job.

Swedish Sand Tarts *(Sandbakelse)*

These tender, buttery-rich dainties are especially popular in Sweden at Christmastime.

1 cup butter
¼ teaspoon almond extract
¾ cup sugar
1 egg
2 cups sifted all-purpose flour
⅓ cup blanched almonds, finely chopped

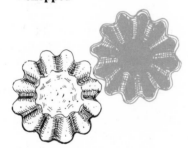

1. Cream butter with extract; add sugar gradually, beating until fluffy. Add egg and beat thoroughly.
2. Add flour in fourths, mixing until blended after each addition. Stir in almonds. Chill dough thoroughly.
3. Remove a small portion of dough at a time from refrigerator and, depending upon size of mold, place 1 or 2 teaspoonfuls in each sandbakelse mold (usually available in the housewares section of department stores); press firmly to cover bottom and sides of mold evenly. Set lined molds on cookie sheets.
4. Bake at 375°F 6 to 8 minutes.
5. Immediately invert molds onto a smooth surface; cool slightly.
6. To remove sand tart, hold mold and tap lightly but sharply with back of spoon. Remove molds and cool cookies. Invert and sift Vanilla Confectioners' Sugar, *page 59,* over cookies.

About 5 dozen cookies

Almond Wreaths *(Mandelkranzchen)*

This rich German cookie is a favorite at Christmastime.

¾ cup butter
½ cup sugar
1 egg
2 cups sifted all-purpose flour
Egg yolk, slightly beaten
½ cup blanched almonds, finely chopped

1. Cream butter; add sugar gradually, beating until fluffy. Add egg and beat thoroughly.
2. Add flour in fourths, mixing until well blended after each addition. Chill dough thoroughly.
3. Roll one half of dough at a time ¼ inch-thick on a floured surface; cut with 1¾-inch round cutter and cut out centers with a ¾-inch round cutter. (Bake centers for samplers.)
4. Transfer rounds and rings to ungreased cookie sheets. Brush tops with egg yolk and sprinkle with almonds.
5. Bake at 350°F 10 to 15 minutes.

About 6 dozen cookies

Pepparkakor

1 **cup butter**
1½ **cups sugar**
1 **egg**
1 **tablespoon dark corn syrup**
2¾ **cups all-purpose flour**
2 **teaspoons baking soda**
1 **tablespoon cinnamon**
2 **teaspoons ginger**
1 **teaspoon ground cloves**
   Blanched almonds
   Icing

1. Beat butter in a bowl until softened. Add sugar gradually, creaming well. Add egg and beat thoroughly. Blend in corn syrup.
2. Blend flour, baking soda, and spices; add to creamed mixture gradually, mixing until blended.
3. Chill dough until easy to handle.
4. Using a portion of the chilled dough at a time, roll dough on a lightly floured surface to ⅛-inch thickness. Cut with floured cookie cutters.
5. Transfer cookies to cookie sheets and decorate some with almonds.
6. Bake at 400°F 5 to 7 minutes. Remove immediately to wire racks.
7. Decorate cooled cookies with icing.

About 6 dozen cookies

Icing: Put **1 egg white** and ⅛ **teaspoon almond extract** into a small bowl. Add **2 cups sifted confectioners' sugar** gradually to egg white while mixing; beat until smooth and glossy.

Holiday Spritz

1 **cup butter**
½ **teaspoon almond extract**
½ **cup sugar**
1 **egg**
2 **cups all-purpose flour**

1. Cream butter with almond extract. Add sugar gradually, creaming well. Add egg and beat thoroughly. Add flour gradually, mixing until blended.
2. Chill dough until easy to handle. Chill cookie press.
3. Following manufacturer's directions, fill cookie press with dough and form cookies of varied shapes directly onto cool ungreased cookie sheets. Decorate with **colored sugar** or **multicolored nonpareil decors.**
4. Bake at 350°F 8 to 10 minutes. Remove to wire racks to cool.

8 to 9 dozen cookies

Semisweet Chocolate Spritz: Melt **2 squares (2 ounces) semisweet chocolate** and set aside to cool. Follow recipe for Holiday Spritz; blend chocolate into creamed mixture. Proceed as directed.

Brandied Apricot Teacakes

8 **ounces dried apricots, chopped**
1 **package (11 ounces) currants**
½ **cup boiling water**
1 **cup apricot brandy**
½ **cup butter**
1½ **cups firmly packed light brown sugar**
3 **eggs**
2 **cups all-purpose flour**
½ **teaspoon baking soda**

1. Put apricots and currants into a bowl; add water and brandy and mix well. Cover and let stand overnight.
2. Beat butter in a large bowl until softened. Add brown sugar gradually, creaming well. Add eggs, one at a time, and beat thoroughly after each addition.
3. Blend flour, baking soda, salt, and spices; add to creamed mixture gradually, mixing well. Blend in fruit mixture.
4. Set midget foil baking cups on baking sheets. Spoon a rounded tablespoonful of mixture into each cup.
5. Bake at 325°F about 30 minutes, or until a wooden pick

½ teaspoon salt
1 teaspoon allspice
1 teaspoon cinnamon
1 teaspoon cloves
Confectioners' sugar

inserted in cake comes out clean. Remove to wire racks to cool.

6. Before serving, sift confectioners' sugar over cakes.

About 5 dozen teacakes

Note: For smaller teacakes without baking cups, use well-buttered 1¾-inch muffin pan wells. Spoon 1 tablespoon mixture into each well. Bake at 325°F about 20 minutes.

About 7 dozen teacakes.

Cookie Strawberries

2 cups butter or margarine (at room temperature)
1 cup confectioners' sugar
2 tablespoons red food coloring
1 tablespoon vanilla extract
4¼ cups all-purpose flour
1 teaspoon salt
2 cups uncooked rolled oats
Frosting

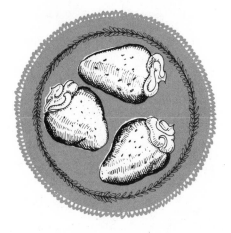

1. Beat butter until creamy. Add confectioners' sugar gradually, beating until smooth. Stir in red food coloring and vanilla extract.
2. Combine flour and salt; add to creamed mixture, blending well. Stir in oats.
3. Shape small pieces of dough to look like strawberries. Gently place wide end (top of strawberry) down on greased cookie sheets.
4. Bake at 325°F about 25 minutes, or until cookies are fairly firm to the touch. Cool.
5. While frosting is warm, dip the top of each "strawberry" in it. Place cookies on wire rack to dry.

About 7 dozen cookies

Frosting: Combine 1⅓ cups sugar, ¼ cup water, and ⅛ teaspoon cream of tartar in a saucepan. Cook to thread stage (about 230°F), or until syrup spins a 2-inch thread when dropped from spoon. While cooking the syrup, beat 2 egg whites until they hold a peak. Pour a stream of hot syrup rapidly into egg whites, beating constantly. After all the syrup is added, continue beating until frosting is very thick and forms rounded peaks (holds shape). Blend in 2 teaspoons green food coloring, 1 teaspoon vanilla extract, and few grains salt.

Norwegian Christmas Cookies (Peppernötter)

1¾ cups sifted all-purpose flour
½ cup cornstarch
2 teaspoons baking powder
½ teaspoon salt
¼ to ½ teaspoon pepper
½ teaspoon ground cardamom
½ teaspoon ground cinnamon
½ teaspoon ground cloves
1 cup butter or margarine
¼ teaspoon vanilla extract
1 cup sugar
¼ cup cream
⅔ cup finely chopped blanched almonds

1. Sift flour, cornstarch, baking powder, salt, and spices together; set aside.
2. Cream butter with extract. Add sugar gradually, beating until light and fluffy.
3. Add dry ingredients alternately with cream, mixing after each addition. Stir in almonds.
4. Shape dough into ¾-inch balls; place 1 inch apart on ungreased cookie sheets.
5. Bake at 350°F about 15 minutes.

About 6 dozen cookies

Anise Form Cookies (Springerle)

These cookies require a special decorative rolling pin or molds to prepare. They're popular at Christmastime in German-speaking countries.

2 eggs
1 cup sugar
½ teaspoon grated lemon peel
8 drops anise oil
2 cups sifted all-purpose flour
¼ teaspoon crushed ammonium carbonate (available at your pharmacy)

1. Beat eggs, sugar, lemon peel, and anise oil until very thick.
2. Blend flour and ammonium carbonate; add in fourths to egg-sugar mixture, mixing until blended after each addition.
3. Cover with a clean towel and let stand at room temperature 1 hour.
4. Shape dough into a ball and, on a floured surface, knead lightly with fingertips; roll ¼ inch thick.
5. Press lightly floured springerle rolling pin or mold firmly into dough to make clear designs.
6. Brush dough surface gently with soft brush to remove excess flour; cut the frames apart; cover and let stand 24 hours.
7. Lightly grease cookie sheets; sprinkle entire surface with **anise seed.**
8. Lightly brush back of each frame with water and set on anise seed.
9. Bake at 325°F 8 minutes.
10. When thoroughly cool, store in a tightly covered container 1 to 2 weeks before serving. To soften cookies, store for several days with a piece of apple or orange.

About 4 dozen cookies

Holiday String-Ups

1 cup butter
2 teaspoons vanilla extract
1½ cups sugar
2 eggs
3¼ cups sifted all-purpose flour
1 teaspoon baking powder
½ teaspoon salt
Confectioners' Sugar Icing, *page 90*

1. Cream butter with extract; add sugar gradually, beating until fluffy. Add eggs, one at a time, beating thoroughly after each addition.
2. Sift flour, baking powder, and salt together; add to creamed mixture in fourths, mixing until blended after each addition. Chill dough thoroughly.
3. Roll a small amount of dough at a time ¼ inch thick on a floured surface; cut into a variety of shapes with cutters. Transfer to ungreased cookie sheets.
4. Insert 1-inch long pieces of paper straws or macaroni into top of each cutout, or press both ends of a piece of colored cord into the dough on the underside of each cutout.
5. Bake at 400°F 6 to 8 minutes.
6. Cool; gently twist out straws, leaving holes for ribbons or cord to be pulled through after decorating.
7. Prepare icing. Color with desired amount of **red** or **green food coloring.** Sprinkle with **decorative sugar.**

About 5 dozen cookies

Note: This versatile dough may be thinly rolled and baked cookies sandwiched together with filling.

Chocolate String-Ups: Follow recipe for Holiday String-Ups. Blend in **2 ounces (2 squares) unsweetened chocolate,** melted and cooled, after the eggs are added. Mix in **1 cup finely chopped pecans** after the last addition of dry ingredients.

Cookies from Around the World

Few of us can travel as often as we'd like, but we can satisfy our wanderlust—partially, at least—by baking up cookies reminiscent of faraway lands. Every country has its own distinctive cookies. This is proof, if any is needed, that cookies are universally popular. Cookie recipes have traveled, sometimes just by word of mouth, from country to country, and have become part of the heritage that one generation passes to the next.

If imitation is the highest form of flattery, Scandinavian cookie bakers have cause for pride. Cookies from Sweden, Denmark, and Norway seem to dominate foreign cookie collections. Scandinavian cookies are often part of holiday cookie baking, and they are a good choice whenever the occasion calls for a cookie that is out of the ordinary.

But every part of the world has its own special cookies. Getting acquainted with them can serve as a short course in ethnic cookery—and the customs of other people. The Chinese delight in the messages tucked inside their fortune cookies. And who knows what sentiments were baked into the Love Letters of Hungary? They lost nothing in translation into the American kitchen.

Cookie recipes have traveled from the far corners of the world, and sometimes they journey back again, in the form of "Care" packages to students or as gifts to loved ones. A few tips to the packer will help insure a safe arrival.

Some cookies are better travelers than others, so it's a good idea to send the ones you know will hold up best. Bars, drops, and fruit cookies are all good choices. Thin, fragile cookies may be able to take the heat in the kitchen, but don't expose them to rough handling.

A few from this chapter that are especially well suited for mailing are the Saskatchewan Orange Glazed Date Bars, Tropical Coconut Jewels, English Toffee Bars, Greek Butter Balls, and Fruity Polish Mazurek.

If the cookies are to be a gift, consider the wrapping suggestions in the holiday chapter. A decorated can that once held potato chips or shortening makes an ideal mailing container, set inside a mailing box and padded with plenty of cushioning material.

If you aren't gift wrapping, stack the cookies carefully and wrap them in plastic film to prevent drying out. Arrange them in layers with crushed tissue paper, unbuttered popcorn, or some other clean packing material in a sturdy carton. It should be so full that you have to press a bit to get the lid on.

Tape the box and give it an outer wrap of heavy paper and cord. Write the address in permanent ink and cover it with transparent tape or clear nail polish. Mark it "Perishable and Fragile"—then send it on its way.

Old-Fashioned Vanilla Sugar Cookies

A Canadian treat.

Vanilla Sugar, *below*
4 cups sifted all-purpose flour
1 teaspoon baking soda
1 teaspoon salt
1 cup shortening
1 tablespoon vanilla extract
2 cups sugar
2 egg yolks
1 cup buttermilk
2 egg whites

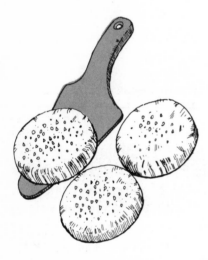

1. Have Vanilla Sugar ready.
2. Sift flour, baking soda, and salt together.
3. Beat shortening with vanilla extract in a large bowl. Add sugar gradually, creaming thoroughly. Beat in egg yolks until mixture is light and fluffy.
4. Alternately add dry ingredients in fourths and buttermilk in thirds to creamed mixture, beating only until blended after each addition.
5. Using a clean beater, beat egg whites until stiff (not dry) peaks are formed. Fold into batter until blended.
6. Drop about 2 tablespoons batter for each cookie onto greased baking sheets, spacing batter 3 inches apart. Using the back of a spoon, spread and shape each into a 2½-inch round ½ inch high. Sprinkle generously with Vanilla Sugar.
7. Bake at 375°F about 15 minutes, or until browned around the edges. Immediately remove to wire racks and sprinkle again with Vanilla Sugar.

About 2½ dozen cookies

Vanilla Sugar: Pour **2 pounds granulated sugar** into a container having a tight-fitting cover. Split a **vanilla bean** in half lengthwise, then cut into 1-inch pieces. Poke pieces down into the sugar at irregular intervals. Cover container tightly and store. The longer the sugar stands, the richer the vanilla flavor. Stir in additional sugar as sugar is used. If tightly covered, sugar may be stored for several months.

Saskatchewan Orange-Glazed Date Bars

1½ cups sifted all-purpose flour
¾ teaspoon baking soda
½ teaspoon salt
¾ cup lightly packed brown sugar
1¼ cups (8 oz.) chopped pitted dates
½ cup water
½ cup soft butter
3 eggs, slightly beaten
½ cup milk
½ cup orange juice
1 cup chopped pecans
Orange Glaze, *below*

1. Sift flour, baking soda, and salt together.
2. Combine brown sugar, dates, and water in a large saucepan. Cook over medium heat, stirring constantly until dates soften. Remove from heat and stir in butter. Add eggs and mix well.
3. Add dry ingredients to date mixture; stir until blended. Add milk and orange juice gradually, mixing well. Stir in nuts.
4. Bake at 350°F about 30 minutes.
5. Cool completely in pan on wire rack. Spread glaze over top and cut into bars.

3 to 4 dozen cookies

Orange Glaze: Combine **2 tablespoons soft butter, 1½ cups sifted confectioners' sugar, 1½ teaspoons grated orange peel, and 2½ tablespoons orange juice;** beat until smooth.

Canadian Oatmeal Drop Cookies

2 cups sifted all-purpose flour
1 cup sugar
1 teaspoon baking soda
1 teaspoon ground cinnamon
½ teaspoon salt
1 cup shortening
1 cup chopped nuts
2½ cups uncooked rolled oats
½ teaspoon grated lemon peel
3 eggs, well beaten
½ cup milk

1. Mix flour, sugar, baking soda, cinnamon, and salt in a bowl. Cut in shortening with a pastry blender or two knives until pieces are the size of rice kernels. Mix in nuts, oats, and lemon peel. Add eggs gradually, mixing thoroughly. Mix in milk thoroughly.
2. Drop by teaspoonfuls about 2 inches apart onto cookie sheets.
3. Bake at 375°F about 10 minutes, or until delicately browned. Cool on wire racks.

About 7½ dozen cookies

Filbert Form Cookies

A Czechoslovakian inspiration.

¾ cup sifted all-purpose flour
⅛ teaspoon baking powder
½ cup confectioners' sugar
¼ teaspoon salt
⅛ teaspoon ground cinnamon
⅛ teaspoon ground cloves
⅛ teaspoon ground nutmeg
½ cup filberts, grated
1 teaspoon grated lemon peel
6 tablespoons butter, chilled

1. Sift flour, baking powder, confectioners' sugar, salt, and spices together; mix in the filberts and lemon peel.
2. Cut in butter until mixture becomes a soft dough (requires working beyond the stage when particles are the size of rice kernels).
3. Cut off small pieces of dough and press into lightly greased fancy 1¼×¼-inch cookie forms (usually available in housewares section of department stores), or half fill lightly greased sandbakelse molds with dough. Set molds on a cookie sheet.
4. Bake at 375°F 10 minutes.
5. Cool about 2 minutes on wire racks. With the point of a knife, loosen cookies from molds; invert onto racks. Sift Vanilla Confectioners' Sugar, *page 59,* over cookies.

About 4 dozen cookies

Pecan Form Cookies: Follow recipe for Filbert Form Cookies. Omit spices and lemon peel. Substitute ⅔ **cup pecans,** grated, for filberts. Mix in **1 teaspoon vanilla extract** with the butter.

Austrian Pecan Cookies

2 tablespoons plus 2 teaspoons
   butter
1½ teaspoons vanilla extract
2 cups firmly packed light brown
   sugar
2 eggs, well beaten
½ cup sifted cake flour
1 teaspoon baking powder
½ teaspoon salt
1½ cups chopped pecans

1. Cream butter with extract; add brown sugar gradually, blending well. Add beaten eggs in halves, beating thoroughly after each addition.
2. Sift cake flour, baking powder, and salt together; add to creamed mixture in halves, mixing until blended after each addition. (Batter will be thin.) Stir in pecans.
3. Drop by teaspoonfuls at least 2 inches apart onto cookie sheets lined with baking parchment.
4. Bake at 375°F about 6 minutes.
5. Cool completely, then remove from paper.

About 10 dozen cookies

Florentines *(Echte Florentiner)*

An Austrian cookie despite its Italian sounding name.

¼ **cup butter**
⅓ **cup firmly packed light brown sugar**
2 **tablespoons honey**
2 **tablespoons light corn syrup**
1 **tablespoon whipping cream**
¾ **cup sifted cake flour**
¼ **teaspoon salt**
1 **cup slivered blanched almonds**
3 **oz. candied orange peel, finely chopped**
Chocolate Glaze I, *page 34;* **triple recipe**

1. Cream butter; add brown sugar gradually, creaming until fluffy. Add honey, corn syrup, and cream gradually, beating well after each addition.
2. Sift flour and salt together; add in thirds to creamed mixture, mixing until blended after each addition. Mix in almonds and candied peel.
3. Drop by level tablespoonfuls 3 inches apart onto greased and lightly floured cookie sheets; spread into 2-inch rounds.
4. Bake at 350°F about 7 minutes. (Cookies should be delicately browned and about 3 inches in diameter with a slightly lacy appearance.)
5. Cool 2 to 3 minutes on cookie sheets. Carefully remove cookies to wire racks; turn flat side up and cool completely.
6. Evenly spread bottom of each cookie with about 1½ teaspoons Chocolate Glaze I. When chocolate is almost set, draw wavy lines through glaze.

About 2 dozen cookies

German Puff Pastry Cookies *(Blätterteig Pastetchen)*

Layer upon tender layer describes these jelly-filled flaky rounds, each with a small "cap."

2 **cups sifted all-purpose flour**
¼ **cup confectioners' sugar**
1 **cup sieved cooked potato, chilled**
1 **cup butter, chilled**
1 **teaspoon vanilla extract**

1. Blend flour and confectioners' sugar; chill.
2. Add potato and mix gently with a fork. Cut in butter until pieces are the size of small peas.
3. Sprinkle extract over mixture, a few drops at a time, mixing lightly with fork (dough should be crumbly). Shape dough into a ball; chill thoroughly.
4. Roll dough, a half at a time, ¼ inch thick on a floured surface; cut with 1¾-inch round cutter and cut centers from half the rounds with a ¾-inch round cutter. Place rounds, rings, and centers on separate ungreased cookie sheets.
5. Bake at 400°F 10 to 15 minutes.
6. When cool, spread rounds with **currant jelly** and top with rings; fill centers of rings with a small amount of jelly; top with centers.

About 2 dozen cookies

Honey Cakes *(Lebkuchen)*

The glaze on this German cookie specialty adds luster and complements the rich, spicy flavor.

3 **cups sifted all-purpose flour**
¼ **teaspoon baking soda**
1 **teaspoon ground cinnamon**
½ **teaspoon ground allspice**
½ **teaspoon ground cloves**

1. Sift flour, baking soda, and spices together; set aside.
2. Beat eggs with sugar until very thick. Add honey gradually, beating well.
3. Add dry ingredients in fourths, folding until blended after each addition. Mix in almonds and candied peels. Turn into a

English Gingered Brandy Snaps, 85

½ teaspoon ground nutmeg
2 eggs
1 cup sugar
½ cup honey
¾ cup unblanched almonds, finely
    chopped
2 oz. candied orange peel, finely
    chopped
2 oz. candied lemon peel, finely
    chopped
Glaze

greased 15×10×1-inch jelly roll pan and spread evenly.
4. Bake at 350°F 25 to 30 minutes.
5. Remove pan to wire rack and cool slightly. Spread Glaze evenly over warm surface. Cut into bars.

About 3 dozen cookies

Glaze: Blend thoroughly ⅓ **cup confectioners' sugar, 1 tablespoon water,** and **1 teaspoon lemon juice.**

Note: More traditionally, Lebkuchen is a rolled cookie which is cut into bars before baking.

German Molasses Cookies

1 cup butter
1¼ cups light molasses
¾ cup firmly packed light brown
    sugar
4 cups sifted all-purpose flour
1 teaspoon baking soda
1 teaspoon salt
2 teaspoons ground ginger
1 teaspoon ground cinnamon
½ to ¾ teaspoon ground cloves

1. Melt butter in a saucepan; add molasses and brown sugar and heat until sugar is dissolved, stirring occasionally. Pour into a bowl; cool.
2. Sift remaining ingredients together; add to cooled mixture in fourths, mixing until blended after each addition.
3. Turn dough onto a floured surface and knead until easy to handle, using additional flour if necessary.
4. Wrap in moisture-vaporproof material; refrigerate and allow dough to ripen one or two days.
5. Roll one fourth of dough at a time about ⅛ inch thick on a floured surface; cut with a 3-inch round cutter or fancy cutters. Transfer to ungreased cookie sheets.
6. Bake at 350°F about 7 minutes.

About 8 dozen cookies

Note: For gingerbread men, roll dough ¼ inch thick and cut with a gingerbread-man cutter. Bake about 13 minutes.

Anise Drops (Anisscheiben)

During baking, these German cookies form a cakelike layer with a crisp "frosting" on the top.

2 extra-large eggs (½ cup)
1 cup sugar
¼ teaspoon anise oil
1⅔ cups sifted all-purpose flour
¼ teaspoon baking powder

1. Beat the eggs, sugar, and anise oil until thick and piled softly.
2. Sift flour and baking powder together; add in fourths to egg-sugar mixture, blending thoroughly after each addition.
3. Drop by teaspoonfuls 2 inches apart onto greased cookie sheets.
4. Set cookie sheets aside in a cool place (not in refrigerator) 8 to 10 hours or overnight. *Do not cover and do not disturb!*
5. Bake at 350°F 5 to 7 minutes.

About 4 dozen cookies

Kolacky Cookies

A Polish treat.

1 cup butter
8 oz. cream cheese, softened
¼ teaspoon vanilla extract
2¼ cups sifted all-purpose flour
½ teaspoon salt
  Cherry preserves, apricot
    preserves, or prune filling

1. Cream butter and cream cheese with extract until fluffy.
2. Blend flour and salt; add in fourths to creamed mixture, mixing until blended after each addition. Chill dough thoroughly.
3. Roll dough ¼ inch thick on a floured surface; cut with 2-inch round cutter or fancy-shaped cutters. Transfer to ungreased cookie sheets, make a small indentation in center of each round, and fill with ½ teaspoon preserves.
4. Bake at 350°F 10 to 15 minutes, or until delicately browned.

About 3½ dozen cookies

Miniature Kolacky

A yeast-raised "sweet" considered a rich bun in some countries. Probably of Czech origin, there are many different versions and spellings of the name.

1 cake (⅝ or ³/₅ oz.) compressed
    yeast
1 cup cream, scalded and cooled
½ teaspoon sugar
3 cups sifted all-purpose flour
⅛ teaspoon salt
1 cup butter, chilled
4 egg yolks
¼ cup sugar
2 teaspoons grated lemon peel
  California or Splendent Filling,
    below

1. Soften yeast in lukewarm cream. Stir in ½ teaspoon sugar and let stand 15 minutes.
2. Blend flour and salt. Cut in the butter with a pastry blender or two knives until particles are the size of rice kernels; set aside.
3. Beat egg yolks and ¼ cup sugar together until very thick. Beat in cream mixture and lemon peel.
4. Make a well in the center of the flour-butter mixture; add egg yolk mixture and blend well. Chill dough overnight.
5. Put half of the chilled dough on a lightly floured surface; roll ¼ inch thick. Cut out rounds with a lightly floured 1½-inch cookie cutter; transfer to ungreased cookie sheets.
6. Make a slight depression in the center of each round and fill with about 1 teaspoonful of filling. Repeat, using remaining dough.
7. Cover and allow to stand in a warm place 10 to 15 minutes.
8. Bake at 350°F 15 to 20 minutes, or until lightly browned. Remove cookies to wire racks.

About 7 dozen kolacky

California Filling

1¼ cups prunes (about 8 oz.), cooked,
    drained, and pitted
¼ cup sugar
2 teaspoons grated lemon peel
3 tablespoons lemon juice

Force prunes through a sieve or food mill. Blend in remaining ingredients; let cool.

1 cup

Splendent Filling

1¼ cups dried apricots, rinsed (about
    8 oz.)

1. Chop apricots and cover with boiling water; cover tightly; simmer 10 to 20 minutes, or until tender.

COOKIES FROM AROUND THE WORLD 83

¾ cup boiling water
½ cup sugar
¼ teaspoon ground cinnamon
2 tablespoons butter

2. Remove from heat; add remaining ingredients and stir until sugar is dissolved and butter is melted. Set aside to cool.

1½ cups

Fruity Polish Mazurek

Delightful small colorful cookie squares—fruity, nutty, and chock-full of wonderful citrus flavor.

2 cups sifted all-purpose flour
1 cup sugar
½ teaspoon salt
½ cup butter or margarine
1 egg
¼ cup half-and-half
1⅔ cups seedless raisins, chopped
1½ cups pitted dates, chopped
1¼ cups dried figs, chopped
1 cup chopped walnuts
⅓ cup sugar
2 eggs
½ cup orange juice
3 tablespoons lemon juice

1. Sift flour, 1 cup sugar, and salt together into a bowl. Cut in butter.
2. Beat egg and cream together and add to flour mixture. Mix lightly with a fork until mixture forms a ball.
3. Spread dough in a greased 15×10×1-inch jelly roll pan.
4. Bake at 350°F about 30 minutes, or until dough is lightly browned around edges.
5. Meanwhile, prepare fruit topping by combining the chopped fruits and walnuts with a mixture of the ⅓ cup sugar, 2 eggs, and fruit juices; mix thoroughly. Spread over partially baked dough in pan.
6. Return to oven and bake 20 minutes.
7. Remove to wire rack; cool. If desired, garnish with **candied fruit** such as candied cherries, candied pineapple, and/or candied orange peel. Cut in 2×1-inch pieces.

About 6 dozen cookies

Italian Butter Cookies (Canestrelli)

4 cups sifted all-purpose flour
1 cup sugar
2½ teaspoons grated lemon peel
1 tablespoon rum
4 egg yolks, beaten
1 cup firm unsalted butter, cut in pieces
1 egg white, slightly beaten

1. Combine flour, sugar, and lemon peel in a large bowl; mix thoroughly. Add rum and then egg yolks in fourths, mixing thoroughly after each addition.
2. Cut butter into flour mixture with pastry blender until particles are fine. Work with fingertips until a dough is formed.
3. Roll one half of dough at a time about ¼ inch thick on a lightly floured surface. Cut into desired shapes. Brush tops with egg white. Transfer to lightly greased cookie sheets.
4. Bake at 350°F about 15 minutes.

About 6 dozen cookies

Grassins

This cookie comes from the Swiss Canton of Grisons, the area where Romansch is spoken, and it is very much like the people, simple and good.

1⅓ cups unsalted butter
1 cup sugar
3 cups sifted all-purpose flour
¼ teaspoon salt
½ teaspoon ground cinnamon

1. Cream butter; add sugar gradually, creaming until fluffy.
2. Sift flour, salt, and cinnamon together; add in fourths to creamed mixture, mixing until blended after each addition.
3. Roll a fourth of dough at a time ¼ inch thick on a floured surface; cut with a 2-inch round cutter. Place on ungreased cookie sheets.
4. Bake at 350°F about 10 minutes.

About 5 dozen cookies

Scottish Shortbread

2 cups sifted all-purpose flour
6 tablespoons sugar
2 tablespoons cornstarch
¾ cup butter

1. Sift flour, sugar, and cornstarch into a bowl. Cut in butter until mixture becomes a soft dough (requires working beyond the stage when particles are the size of rice kernels).
2. Shape dough into a ball; knead lightly with fingertips until mixture holds together.
3. Roll half of the dough at a time ¼ to ½ inch thick on a floured surface.
4. Cut into 1½×½-inch strips, or use fancy cutters. Place on ungreased cookie sheets.
5. Bake at 350°F 25 to 30 minutes; do not brown.

2½ to 4 dozen cookies

Petticoat Tails: Follow recipe for Scottish Shortbread. Roll dough about ¼ inch thick; cut out 5- or 6-inch rounds and cut a 2½-inch round from the center of each. (Bake centers for samplers.) Cut each ring into 8 pieces; crimp all edges of each piece and prick the surface with a fork; bake as directed.

Grasmere Shortbread: Follow recipe for Scottish Shortbread. Blend ½ **teaspoon ground ginger** with dry ingredients. After addition of butter, stir in ½ **cup finely chopped crystallized ginger.** Roll a fourth of dough at a time ⅛ inch thick on a floured surface; cut with a 2-inch fluted round cutter. Bake on ungreased cookie sheets at 350°F 12 minutes. Cool. Spread **Ginger Filling,** *below,* over bottoms of half the cooled cookies; cover with remaining cookies.

About 3 dozen cookies

Ginger Filling: Cream ¼ **cup butter** and **1 teaspoon vanilla extract;** add **2 cups confectioners' sugar** gradually, beating until fluffy. Stir in **1 tablespoon milk** until of spreading consistency. Stir in **2 tablespoons grated crystallized ginger.**

About ⅔ cup

Edinburgh Squares

Melt-in-your-mouth, nut-rich layer, covered with jelly topped with chocolate meringue, results in taste-tempting squares you'll make often.

1½ cups sifted all-purpose flour
¼ cup sugar
½ cup butter, chilled
¾ cup unblanched almonds, grated (2 cups)
2 egg yolks, well beaten
1½ tablespoons currant jelly or apricot preserves
1 egg white
⅛ teaspoon cream of tartar
¼ cup sugar
1½ oz. sweet chocolate, melted and cooled

1. Blend flour and ¼ cup sugar. Cut in butter until pieces are the size of small peas. Blend in 1½ cups of the grated almonds. Add egg yolks and mix thoroughly.
2. Shape dough into a ball, kneading lightly with fingertips; put onto an ungreased cookie sheet; roll into a 10½×7½-inch rectangle. Spread evenly with jelly; set aside.
3. Beat egg white and cream of tartar until frothy; gradually add ¼ cup sugar, continuing to beat until stiff peaks are formed.
4. Gently fold in cooled chocolate and remaining grated almonds; spread evenly over jelly-topped dough.
5. Bake at 300°F 25 to 30 minutes.
6. When cool, cut into squares.

About 3 dozen cookies

English Toffee Bars

1 cup butter
1 cup sugar
1 egg yolk
2 cups sifted all-purpose flour
1 teaspoon ground cinnamon
1 egg white, slightly beaten
1 cup chopped pecans
2 oz. (2 sq.) semisweet chocolate, melted

1. Cream butter; add sugar gradually, beating until fluffy. Beat in egg yolk.
2. Sift the flour and cinnamon together; gradually add to creamed mixture, beating until blended.
3. Turn into a greased 15×10×1-inch jelly roll pan and press evenly. Brush top with egg white. Sprinkle with pecans and press lightly into dough.
4. Bake at 275°F 1 hour.
5. While still hot, cut into 1½-inch squares. Drizzle with melted chocolate. Cool on wire rack.

5 to 6 dozen cookies

English Gingered Brandy Snaps

¼ cup butter or margarine
¼ cup sugar
2 tablespoons light corn syrup
1 teaspoon molasses
½ cup all-purpose flour
½ teaspoon ground ginger
⅛ teaspoon ground nutmeg
1 tablespoon brandy

Filling:
1 cup whipping cream, whipped
1 tablespoon sugar

1. Combine butter, sugar, corn syrup, and molasses in a medium saucepan. Heat mixture over medium heat just until butter is melted.
2. Combine flour, ginger, and nutmeg in a small bowl. Stir this mixture into the butter mixture. Stir in the brandy.
3. Drop the mixture by teaspoonfuls 6 inches apart on greased cookie sheets.
4. Bake at 350°F 8 to 10 minutes. Let cool for 30 seconds. Ease cookies off the cookie sheet with a spatula; then immediately roll loosely around a 6-inch tapered metal tube with the upper surface of each brandy snap on the outside. Cool on wire racks.
5. Shortly before serving, whip cream, add sugar, and mix well. Using a pastry bag fitted with a star tip, fill the cavity in the rolled brandy snap from each end.

15 cookies

Note: If brandy snaps begin to harden before they are rolled, return them to the oven for 30 seconds to soften them.

Shrewsbury Biscuits

Americans would call these tender, currant-flecked treats cookies, but being an English favorite, they're biscuits.

¾ cup butter
2 teaspoons grated lemon peel
2 tablespoons lemon juice
¾ cup sugar
1 egg
1¾ cups sifted all-purpose flour
½ teaspoon baking powder
¼ teaspoon salt
1 cup currants

1. Cream butter with lemon peel and juice; add sugar gradually, beating until fluffy. Add egg and beat thoroughly.
2. Sift flour, baking powder, and salt together; add in fourths to creamed mixture, mixing until blended after each addition. Mix in currants. Chill dough thoroughly.
3. Roll a third of dough at a time ¼ inch thick on a floured surface. Cut with 2½-inch fluted cutter. Brush cutouts with **milk;** sprinkle with **sugar.** Transfer to ungreased cookie sheets.
4. Bake at 350°F 12 to 15 minutes.

About 2½ dozen cookies

Greek Butter Ball Cookies (Kourabiedes)

3 cups sifted cake flour
¼ teaspoon baking soda
¾ cup chopped blanched almonds, crushed with rolling pin
1 cup unsalted butter
1 tablespoon sugar
1½ teaspoons brandy
½ teaspoon lemon juice
Few drops almond extract
1 teaspoon olive oil
1 large egg yolk, fork beaten
Confectioners' sugar

1. Mix the flour, baking soda, and almonds; set aside.
2. Heat butter slowly in a small deep saucepan. Cool. Carefully spoon off into a large bowl the clarified butter from top of cloudy solids which have settled at bottom of pan.
3. Add sugar, brandy, lemon juice, extract, oil, and egg yolk to butter; beat well. Add the flour-nut mixture in fourths, mixing thoroughly after each addition.
4. Shape dough into ¾-inch balls and place on ungreased cookie sheets.
5. Bake at 350°F 15 minutes.
6. Meanwhile, line a jelly roll pan with absorbent paper and generously sift confectioners' sugar over paper. Remove cookies carefully to the sugar and roll gently to coat. Transfer to cookie jar when cool.

About 4 dozen cookies

Chinese Almond Cookies

Typical of the well-known almond cookies served in Chinese restaurants.

2½ cups blanched almonds
2¼ cups sifted all-purpose flour
1¼ cups butter
1¼ cups sugar

1. Finely chop 1⅔ cups almonds; toast remaining almonds, if desired, and set aside for garnish.
2. Mix flour and chopped almonds; set aside.
3. Cream butter; add sugar gradually, beating thoroughly.
4. Add flour-nut mixture gradually, mixing until blended after each addition.
5. Divide dough into thirds, wrap in waxed paper, and chill until easy to handle.
6. Shape dough into 1-inch balls; place about 2 inches apart on ungreased cookie sheets and flatten each until about ½ inch thick. Press a whole almond onto the top of each.
7. Bake at 325°F 10 to 15 minutes.
8. Immediately remove cookies to wire racks.

About 6 dozen cookies

Note: Firmly packed light brown sugar may be substituted for the granulated sugar.

Dutch Almond Cookies

2 cups sifted all-purpose flour
1 teaspoon baking powder
¼ teaspoon salt
1 cup firmly packed dark brown sugar
½ teaspoon ground nutmeg
¼ teaspoon ground cinnamon
1 cup butter
½ cup milk
½ lb. blanched almonds, ground
1 cup sugar
1 tablespoon grated lemon peel
1 egg, slightly beaten

1. Blend flour, baking powder, salt, brown sugar, nutmeg, and cinnamon; cut in butter until particles are the size of rice kernels. Add milk and stir until blended.
2. Spoon half of mixture into an ungreased 11×7×1½-inch baking pan and spread evenly; set aside.
3. Mix remaining ingredients well. Turn mixture onto waxed paper and shape into an even layer the size of the pan. Invert over layer in pan and peel off paper. Spoon remaining mixture over almond layer and spread evenly.
4. Bake at 350°F 45 minutes.
5. Cut into bars while warm; cool completely before removing from pan.

About 2 dozen cookies

Spanish Butter Wafers (Mantecaditos)

½ cup butter
½ cup lard
1½ teaspoons grated lemon peel, or 1 teaspoon anise seed (or both)
1 teaspoon vanilla extract
1¼ cups sugar
2 eggs
1¾ cups sifted all-purpose flour
½ teaspoon salt

1. Cream butter and lard with lemon peel and extract. Add sugar gradually, beating until fluffy. Add eggs, one at a time, beating thoroughly after each addition.
2. Blend flour and salt; add to creamed mixture in thirds, mixing until blended after each addition. Chill dough several hours, or until easy to handle.
3. Removing a small portion of dough at a time from refrigerator, shape into ¾- to 1-inch balls and place 1½ inches apart on an ungreased cookie sheet.
4. Bake at 350°F 8 to 10 minutes.

6 to 7 dozen cookies

Hungarian Butter Cookies

2¾ cups sifted all-purpose flour
3 teaspoons baking powder
¼ teaspoon salt
1½ cups unsalted butter, chilled
4 egg yolks, slightly beaten
1 cup dairy sour cream
¼ cup sugar
1 egg white, slightly beaten

1. Sift flour, baking powder, and salt together into a bowl. Cut in butter until particles are the size of rice kernels.
2. Add a mixture of egg yolks, sour cream, and sugar, mixing until blended.
3. Knead until a smooth dough is formed.
4. Roll dough ¼ inch thick on a lightly floured surface; cut with a 2½-inch round cutter.
5. With a sharp knife make a crisscross pattern on top of each; brush with egg white and sprinkle lightly with Vanilla Granulated Sugar, *page 78.* Place on ungreased cookie sheets.
6. Bake at 400°F 5 minutes. Reduce oven temperature to 350°F and bake about 14 minutes.

About 4 dozen cookies

Swedish Jelly Slices

¾ cup butter
1 teaspoon grated lemon peel
¾ cup sugar
1 egg
1¾ cups sifted all-purpose flour
1½ teaspoons baking powder
¼ teaspoon salt
1 teaspoon ground coriander
½ teaspoon ground cardamom
1 jar (10 ounces) red cherry jelly
1 egg yolk
¼ cup sugar
2 teaspoons water
¼ cup finely chopped toasted blanched almonds

1. Cream butter with lemon peel. Add ¾ cup sugar gradually, creaming thoroughly. Add egg and beat well.
2. Blend flour, baking powder, salt, and spices; add to creamed mixture and mix well.
3. Chill dough until easy to handle.
4. On a floured surface, roll dough into a 12×8-inch rectangle. Cut into 12 (1-inch) strips.
5. Place strips 4 inches apart on greased cookie sheets; cookies will spread. Make a depression, ¼ inch wide and ¼ inch deep, lengthwise down the center of each strip of dough. Fill depressions with jelly.
6. Bake at 375°F 10 minutes.
7. Meanwhile, combine egg yolk, ¼ cup sugar, and water and beat until thick.
8. Remove cookies from oven. Brush egg yolk mixture on hot cookies and sprinkle with almonds. Return cookies to oven and bake 5 minutes.
9. Cool cookies 5 minutes on cookie sheets. Add more jelly, if desired. Cut diagonally into 1-inch slices. Cool on wire racks.

About 7 dozen cookies

Swedish Coffee Fingers (Mördegspinnar)

½ cup butter
1 teaspoon almond extract
2 tablespoons sugar
1¼ cups sifted all-purpose flour
    Egg white, slightly beaten
½ cup finely chopped blanched
    almonds
3 tablespoons sugar

1. Cream butter with extract; add 2 tablespoons sugar gradually, beating until fluffy.
2. Add flour in fourths, mixing until blended after each addition. Chill dough thoroughly.
3. Shape small amounts of dough into fingers 2½ inches long and ¼ inch thick.
4. Brush each finger of dough with the egg white, then roll in mixture of the almonds and the remaining sugar.
5. Bake on ungreased cookie sheets at 350°F 10 to 12 minutes.
6. Carefully remove cookies to wire racks.

About 5 dozen cookies

Scandinavian Springerle

Unlike the firm anise-flavored German Springerle, this delicately spiced cookie is pleasingly tender.

2 cups sifted all-purpose flour
½ teaspoon ground cardamom
½ teaspoon ground cinnamon
1 cup butter
1 cup confectioners' sugar
¾ cup blanched almonds, finely
    chopped

1. Sift flour and spices together; set aside.
2. Cream butter; add confectioners' sugar gradually, beating until fluffy. Add flour mixture in fourths, mixing until well blended after each addition. Stir in almonds. Chill dough thoroughly.
3. Roll dough ¼ inch thick on a floured surface or between sheets of waxed paper. Press lightly floured springerle rolling pin firmly into dough, rolling carefully to make clear designs; or press individual springerle molds firmly into dough.
4. Brush surface of dough gently with a soft brush to remove excess flour; cut the frames apart. Transfer to ungreased cookie sheets.
5. Bake at 350°F 10 minutes.

About 2½ dozen cookies

Swedish Doughnut Miniatures

1½ cups sifted all-purpose flour
1 teaspoon baking powder
    Few grains salt
1 egg
⅓ cup sugar
1 teaspoon vanilla extract
1½ teaspoons grated lemon peel, or ½
    to ¾ teaspoon ground
    cardamom
⅓ cup half-and-half
2 tablespoons butter or margarine,
    melted
    Fat for deep frying heated to
    375°F

1. Sift flour, baking powder, and salt together.
2. Beat egg, sugar, extract, and lemon peel together until thick and piled softly. (If using cardamom, blend with flour.)
3. Alternately add dry ingredients in halves with mixture of cream and butter, beating until just blended after each addition. Chill dough if necessary for easier handling.
4. Roll dough to ¼-inch thickness on a floured surface. Cut dough with a lightly floured 2¼-inch scalloped cutter and use a small round cutter (about ½ inch) to cut out center.
5. Fry in hot fat about 2 minutes, or until golden brown, turning immediately as doughnuts rise to surface and several times during cooking.
6. Remove from fat with a slotted spoon and drain on absorbent paper. Coat doughnuts with **sugar.** Serve while warm.

About 1½ dozen cookies

Scandinavian Walnut Cookies

1 cup butter or margarine
½ cup sugar
1 teaspoon vanilla extract
2¼ cups sifted all-purpose flour
½ cup finely chopped walnuts

1. Cream butter, sugar, and vanilla extract together until well blended. Gradually blend in flour to make a stiff dough.
2. Mix in the walnuts; omit walnuts if preparing Finnish Bread. Shape and bake as below.

Finnish Bread: Using about 1 tablespoon of dough at a time, shape dough into small rolls 2¼ inches long, and place on lightly greased cookie sheet. Brush tops of cookies with **slightly beaten egg white** and sprinkle with **½ cup chopped walnuts.** Bake at 350°F 15 to 18 minutes.

About 30 cookies

Grandma's Jelly Cookies: Roll dough a little less than ¼ inch thick, and cut out rounds using a 2-inch cutter. Cut a circle from the center of half of the rounds. Place rounds on lightly greased cookie sheets and bake at 350°F 10 to 12 minutes. When completely cool, spread ¾ **teaspoon tart jelly** on each of the solid rounds and top with a round with a cutout center.

About 40 double cookies

Walnut Balls: Shape dough into balls 1¼ inches in diameter. Chill thoroughly before baking, so balls will hold their shape. Bake at 350°F 25 minutes. Balls may be rolled in **powdered sugar** while hot, and again when cold. Or cool balls on wire rack and frost tops of balls with **powdered sugar frosting** when completely cooled.

About 2½ dozen cookies

Frosted Triangles: Divide dough into 4 portions. Roll one portion of dough at a time into a strip 12 inches long and 1¾ inches wide. Transfer strip to a greased cookie sheet. Bake at 350°F 20 minutes. Cool slightly on cookie sheet, then carefully slide onto wire rack to cool completely. When cold, make a ruffle of frosting down the center of each strip, using your favorite buttercream frosting and a pastry bag fitted with a star tip. Cut into triangles when frosting is set.

About 32 triangles

Jam Slices: Divide dough into four portions and roll into 12-inch strips as described for Frosted Triangles. Transfer strips to cookie sheet. With a finger, press a slight depression down the center of the entire length of the strip. Fill the depression using **2 tablespoons apricot jam** for each strip. Sprinkle each strip with **1 tablespoon finely chopped walnuts.** Bake at 350°F about 20 minutes. Cool slightly on cookie sheet, then slide carefully onto a wire rack, using broad spatulas. Cut in diagonal slices when cold. (Note: These cookies soften on standing, from moisture in jam, so are best eaten within a day or two of baking.)

About 32 slices

Medallion Cookies (Medaljakager)

This Danish cream-filled frosted cookie may be served in pairs on individual plates and eaten with a fork as dessert.

Cream Filling, *below*
2 cups butter
1 cup confectioners' sugar
1 egg
4¼ cups sifted all-purpose flour
Confectioners' Sugar Icing, *below*

1. Prepare filling and chill.
2. Cream butter; add confectioners' sugar gradually, beating until fluffy. Add egg; beat thoroughly.
3. Add flour in fourths, mixing until blended after each addition. Cover and set aside 20 minutes (do not refrigerate).
4. Roll a third of the dough at a time ¼ inch thick on a floured surface; cut with 2-inch round cutter. Transfer to ungreased cookie sheets.
5. Bake at 375°F about 10 minutes.
6. Spread about ¾ teaspoon filling over bottom of each of half the cooled cookies; top with remaining cookies; spread icing over tops.

About 5 dozen cookies

Note: The cookies should be filled shortly before serving time. Fill only as many cookies as will be needed. Refrigerate the filled cookies if they are to be held for any length of time.

Cream Filling

⅓ cup sugar
2 tablespoons flour
⅛ teaspoon salt
1 cup milk
2 egg yolks, slightly beaten
1 tablespoon butter
1 teaspoon vanilla extract

1. Mix sugar, flour, and salt in a double-boiler top. Add the milk gradually, stirring until blended. Stirring constantly, bring mixture rapidly to boiling; boil 3 minutes.
2. Vigorously stir about 3 tablespoons of the hot mixture into the egg yolks; immediately blend into mixture in the double boiler.
3. Cook over simmering water 3 to 5 minutes, stirring constantly.
4. Stir in the butter and extract. Cool slightly; chill.

About 1 cup

Confectioners' Sugar Icing: Combine **1 cup confectioners' sugar** and **½ teaspoon vanilla extract**. Blend in **milk or cream** (about 1 tablespoon) until icing is of spreading consistency.

About 1 cup

Note: To tint, blend in **1 or 2 drops food coloring**.

Brown Wafers

Spices and orange peel lend a pleasing flavor blend to this Danish cookie.

1 cup butter
1¼ cups sugar
½ cup light corn syrup
2½ teaspoons crushed ammonium carbonate (available at your pharmacy)
3 tablespoons ground cinnamon
½ teaspoon ground cloves

1. Heat butter, sugar, and corn syrup to boiling in a heavy saucepan; stir to blend. Cool.
2. Stir a small amount of **cold water** (about 1 teaspoon) into the ammonium carbonate. Blend into cooled butter mixture.
3. Add spices, almonds, and orange peel, stirring only enough to blend the ingredients.
4. Add the flour in thirds, stirring until blended after each addition; mix well.

½ cup slivered almonds
½ cup finely shredded orange peel
4 cups sifted all-purpose flour

5. Shape the dough into four 2¼-inch rolls. Wrap in moisture-vaporproof material; chill overnight or longer.
6. Cut each roll into thin slices. Transfer slices to greased cookie sheets.
7. Bake at 350°F 5 to 7 minutes.
8. Store cookies in a loosely covered container.

About 8 dozen cookies

Brown Sugar Cookies (Brunekager)

A simply delicious Danish cookie.

1 cup butter
¾ cup firmly packed brown sugar
1 egg yolk
2 cups sifted all-purpose flour
Pecan halves

1. Cream butter; add brown sugar gradually, beating until fluffy. Beat in egg yolk thoroughly.
2. Add flour in fourths, mixing until blended after each addition.
3. Shape dough into ½- to ¾-inch balls; place balls 2 inches apart on ungreased cookie sheets. Flatten with a lightly floured fork, making a crisscross design on the tops. Press a pecan half onto center of each.
4. Bake at 375°F 8 to 10 minutes.

About 7 dozen cookies

Danish Saddle Cookies (Krumkager)

Baked rectangularly shaped butter cookies are gently curved (while still warm) over wooden sticks to form "saddles." The youngsters will love them!

½ cup finely chopped blanched almonds
¼ cup sugar
1 cup butter or margarine
1 cup plus 2 tablespoons sugar
2¼ cups sifted all-purpose flour
2 egg yolks, beaten
1 tablespoon water

1. Save 1- to 1¼-inch-diameter cardboard rollers from paper toweling or moisture-vaporproof material and cover with aluminum foil. Use these to form the saddle cookies.
2. Mix almonds and the ¼ cup sugar; set aside.
3. Cream butter; gradually add the remaining sugar, beating well. Add flour in fourths, mixing until well blended after each addition.
4. Working with a small amount of dough at a time, roll out into a rectangle about ¼ inch thick on a lightly floured surface. Cut into 3×1½-inch rectangles. Place on ungreased cookie sheets.
5. Brush tops of cookies with a mixture of the beaten egg yolks and water. Sprinkle with the almond-sugar mixture.
6. Bake at 375°F 3 to 10 minutes, or until delicately browned.
7. Cool cookies slightly on sheets, remove and bend lengthwise over foil-wrapped rollers to cool. Carefully remove cooled cookies.

About 7 dozen cookies

Vanilla Rings

A rich Danish cookie.

1 cup butter
1 vanilla bean, split lengthwise and pulp removed (about ½ teaspoon)
2 cups sifted all-purpose flour
¾ cup sugar
1½ tablespoons slightly beaten egg

1. Cream butter with vanilla bean pulp. Add flour in halves, mixing thoroughly after each addition. Add sugar gradually, beating well. Mix in egg and continue beating just until smooth. Chill at least 2 hours.
2. Removing only a small amount of dough at a time from refrigerator, transfer to a bowl set in a bowl of ice and water. For each ring, roll (working quickly) about ½ teaspoon dough between palms of hands to 3 or 4 inches in length and about ¼ inch thickness. Place on lightly greased cookie sheet, joining ends to form a ring. Chill palms of hands between each rolling by holding them against sides of bowl.
3. Bake at 400°F 6 to 8 minutes.

About 9 dozen cookies

Danish Peppernuts (Pebernødder)

The Danes have achieved an especially fine blend of flavors with sugar and spices and good Danish butter in this version of Pebernødder.

4 cups sifted all-purpose flour
1 teaspoon crushed ammonium carbonate (available at your pharmacy)
1½ teaspoons ground cinnamon
1 teaspoon white pepper
1 teaspoon ground ginger
¾ cup butter
4 teaspoons finely shredded lemon peel
1¼ cups sugar
2 eggs
¾ cup finely chopped almonds

1. Thoroughly blend flour, ammonium carbonate, cinnamon, white pepper, and ginger; set aside.
2. Cream butter with lemon peel. Add sugar gradually, beating until fluffy. Add eggs, one at a time, beating well after each addition. Stir in almonds.
3. Add dry ingredients in thirds, mixing until blended after each addition. Chill about 1 hour.
4. Shape dough into ¾- to 1-inch balls; place on ungreased cookie sheets.
5. Bake at 350°F 12 or 13 minutes.

About 12 dozen cookies

Tiny Doughnut Cookies (Jortitog)

This is one of Norway's fine cookies—more like "fried cake" than cookie.

½ cup butter
1 cup sugar
4 eggs
3 cups sifted all-purpose flour
½ teaspoon crushed ammonium carbonate (available at your pharmacy)
½ teaspoon salt
Fat for deep frying heated to 375°F

1. Cream butter; add sugar gradually, beating until fluffy. Add eggs, one at a time, beating thoroughly after each addition.
2. Blend flour, ammonium carbonate, and salt; add in fourths to creamed mixture, mixing until blended after each addition. Chill dough at least 1 hour.
3. Roll a fourth of dough at a time ¼ inch thick on a floured surface; cut into 2×½-inch strips.
4. Roll each strip 3 inches long; bring ends together to form ring and press to seal; make 3 slanted cuts at equal intervals around each. Let dry about 1 minute.
5. Deep fry in hot fat 1 to 2 minutes, or until lightly browned; turn once.
6. Drain; serve while still warm.

About 16 dozen cookies

Toasted Cakes *(Kanelbröd)*

Some call these tender, spicy toasted slices bread, others cake. No matter what the name, these Danish treats are bound to bring "raves" from your friends when you accompany the golden morsels with piping hot coffee at a special brunch.

4 cups sifted all-purpose flour
2 tablespoons baking powder
1 teaspoon ground cinnamon
1 cup sugar
1 cup butter
3 eggs, well beaten

1. Sift flour, baking powder, cinnamon, and sugar together into a bowl. Cut in butter until particles are fine.
2. Add eggs in thirds, mixing until blended after each addition.
3. Shape into 2 loaves about 12×1½ inches; place on an ungreased cookie sheet.
4. Bake at 350°F 30 minutes.
5. Immediately cut loaves diagonally into ½-inch slices. Toast slices in oven about 4 minutes on each side.

About 5 dozen cookies

Danish Knots *(Kringler)*

2¼ cups sifted all-purpose flour
1 tablespoon sugar
1 teaspoon baking powder
½ cup firm butter
1 cup chilled whipping cream, whipped
Crushed loaf sugar

1. Sift flour, sugar, and baking powder together into a bowl. Cut in butter until particles are the size of rice kernels.
2. Mix in cream with a fork and knead lightly with fingertips until mixture makes a ball.
3. Roll a fourth of dough at a time into a 6×4-inch rectangle ¼-inch thick on a floured surface. Sprinkle crushed loaf sugar over the dough, pressing in lightly. Cut into 6×¼-inch strips. Form into figure eights or loose knots to resemble pretzels. Place on ungreased cookie sheets.
4. Bake at 400°F about 12 minutes.

About 5 dozen cookies

Berlin Wreaths *(Berlinerkranser)*

A Norwegian specialty.

1 cup butter
½ teaspoon vanilla extract
½ cup sugar
2 uncooked egg yolks
3 hard-cooked egg yolks, sieved
2 cups sifted all-purpose flour

1. Cream butter with extract; add sugar gradually, beating until fluffy.
2. Add uncooked egg yolks, one at a time, beating thoroughly after each addition; mix in hard-cooked egg yolks.
3. Add flour in fourths, mixing until blended after each addition. Chill dough thoroughly.
4. Shape small amounts of dough into strips 4 inches long and ¼ inch thick; the ends of strips should be slightly pointed. Form wreaths on ungreased cookie sheets, overlapping ends of strips about ¼ inch.
5. Brush wreaths with slightly beaten **egg white**; sprinkle lightly with crushed **loaf sugar.**
6. Bake at 350°F 10 to 12 minutes.

About 5 dozen cookies

Index